Women's Dionysian Initiation

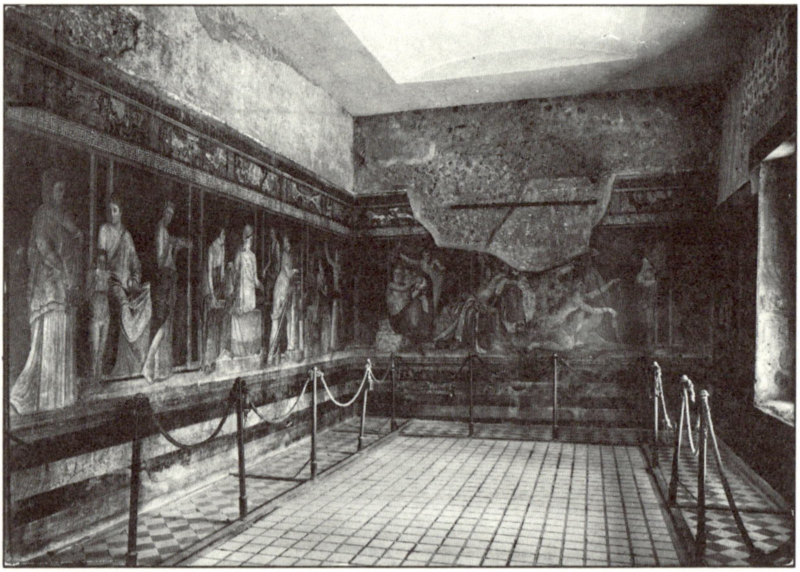

The Hall of the Villa of Mysteries in Pompeii

Women's Dionysian Initiation
The Villa of Mysteries in Pompeii

LINDA FIERZ-DAVID

Translated by Gladys Phelan
and with an Introduction by
M. Esther Harding

Spring Publications, Inc.
Dallas, Texas

Jungian Classics Series 11
Published 1988 by Spring Publications, Inc.;
P.O. Box 222069; Dallas, Texas 75222.
Printed in the United States of America

Gladys Phelan's translation is of the work *Psychologische Betrachtungen zu der Freskenfolge der Villa dei Misteri in Pompeii: Ein Versuch*, mimeographed in Zürich, Switzerland, 1957, © by the Psychological Club of Zürich.
Mimeographing of the German study was made possible in the memory of Linda Fierz-David by her sons: Markus, Heinrich, Felix and Niklaus Fierz.
International distributors:
Spring; Postfach; 8803 Ruschlikon; Switzerland.
Japan Spring Sha, Inc.; 12-10, 2-Chome, Nigawa Takamaru; Takarazuka 665, Japan.
Element Books Ltd; Longmead Shaftesbury; Dorset SP7 8PL; England.

Library of Congress Cataloging-in-Publication Data

Fierz-David, Linda.
Women's Dionysian initiation.

(Jungian classics series ; 11)
Translation of: Psychologische Betrachtungen zu der Freskenfolge der Villa dei Misteri in Pompeii.
Bibliography: p.
1. Villa of the Mysteries frescoes (Mural painting) 2. Mural painting and decoration – Italy – Pompeii (Ancient city) 3. Dionysus (Greek deity) – Art. 4. Villa of the Mysteries (Pompeii) 5. Pompeii (Ancient city) – Buildings, structures, etc. 6. Dionysia in art. 7. Mysteries, Religious, in art. 8. Women – Psychology. 9. Jung, C. G. (Carl Gustav), 1875-1961 – Criticism and interpretation. 10. Italy – Antiquities. I. Title. II. Series.
ND2575.F513 1988 755'.9238'09377 88-4893
ISBN 0-88214-510-X (pbk.)

Contents

Acknowledgments vii
Preface by H. K. Fierz ix
Introduction by M. Esther Harding xi

Entering the Villa

History of the Villa of Mysteries 3
The Initiation Chamber 10
The Mythological Hypothesis of the Mystery Cult: Dionysus and Ariadne 18

The Sacred Drama in the Villa of Mysteries

The First Scene 33
The Second Scene 36
The Third Scene 51
The Fourth and Fifth Scenes 66
The Sixth Scene 86
The Seventh Scene 88
The Eighth Scene 119
The Ninth and Tenth Scenes 138

Notes 145
Publisher's Note 149

Acknowledgments

Spring Publications, Inc., gratefully acknowledges the following:

The cooperation of the C. G. Jung Foundation for Analytical Psychology of New York in making possible publication of this translation – which it originally commissioned – and including the introduction by M. Esther Harding.

Scala/Art Resource, N.Y., for the artwork used to reproduce the color plates of the frescoes in the Villa dei Misteri, Pompeii.

Mary Vernon for her drawing of the fig, used throughout these pages.

Catherine Meehan Doehner and Sven Doehner for designing and producing the cover.

Nor Hall, for providing the photograph reproduced as the frontispiece.

Permission of Princeton University Press for reprinting extracts from the following volumes of *The Collected Works of C. G. Jung,* trans. R. F. C. Hull, Bollingen Series XX:

Vol. 9, ii: *Aion: Researches into the Phenomenology of the Self,* copyright © 1959 by Princeton University Press.

Vol. 11: *Psychology and Religion: West and East,* copyright © 1958, 1969 by Princeton University Press.

Vol. 12: *Psychology and Alchemy*, copyright © 1953, © 1968 by Princeton University Press.

Vol. 13: *Alchemical Studies*, copyright © 1967 by Princeton University Press.

Vol. 16: *The Practice of Psychotherapy,* copyright 1954, © 1966 by Princeton University Press.

Preface

Until her death in 1955, Linda Fierz-David was a docent at the C. G. Jung Institute, Zürich. She devoted her last lectures to the fresco series in the Villa of Mysteries in Pompeii. The work which arose from these lectures, and which she was able to complete before her death, she rightly described as "psychological reflections." This is a psychological work and is not concerned with research into antiquity. It is the typical primeval experience of a human being who, instead of looking at the frescoes in the Villa of Mysteries esthetically or archaeologically, experiences the psychic reality radiating from them.

This sort of intense psychic experience is the central concern of psychology. It opens our eyes to the dynamic of the psyche, to the ever-present and yet timeless archetypal associations. "Psychological reflections" cannot assume an unmoved and untouched observer. The state of being seized by a psychic content is intensely personal. Therefore it does not seem advisable to revise these "psychological reflections" in order to bring them into accord with the latest discoveries of classical research. Such a revision could only impair their psychological importance.

Linda Fierz-David's work is therefore published exactly as the author herself concluded it.

Heinrich Karl Fierz
Zürich, 1966

Introduction

Anyone who has stood, as I have, in the Initiation Hall of the Villa of Mysteries, outside the north wall of Pompeii, cannot but have been impressed by the simplicity and beauty of the pictures painted on the four walls of the room. Each scene represents one or, perhaps, two or three figures. The designs are seemingly simple, yet obviously they portray a sequence of events that forms a complex, coherent drama. Some of the figures give the impression of being portraits of contemporary persons – they are obviously real human beings – while others have a mythological character and yet play a part in the pictured drama as though they, too, were contemporary persons and were as actual and as materially present as the others.

The reality of the main figures makes it clear that the series is not merely the representation of a myth, but is rather intended to portray the inner or psychological reality of certain mythic happenings, as they might be represented by one undergoing a profound psychological experience in which the background material and drama which are usually entirely unconscious are activated. We ordinarily experience such things only in dreams, but under certain circumstances the "stuff as dreams are made on" appears before the inner eye as if it were objectively real and really happening. Such experiences do have an emotional reality, and they can affect the individuals profoundly, perhaps causing a deep and permanent transformation of their personality.

The experience portrayed on the walls of the Villa represents such an inner ritual, whose counterpart can be observed today only as a secret and subjective happening of an entirely psychological nature. Like the mystery initiation, this inner experience can have profound effects on an individual's life and character.

Professor Maiuri, in his *Villa dei Misteri,* gives a detailed description of these paintings and shows how they correspond to a ritual of initiation as it was enacted in the years of the first century B.C. He comes to the conclusion that, although in many ways the rituals portrayed probably correspond to the initiation mysteries practiced at Eleusis, they probably concerned the little-known Dionysiac or Orphic rites. The central figures on the narrow back wall of the chamber are drawn on a different and larger scale than the other figures of the series. Unfortunately they are badly damaged, but Maiuri is of the opinion that they represent the god Dionysus and Ariadne in their embrace on the island of Naxos, where Ariadne, in inconsolable grief at her desertion by Theseus, is about to commit suicide. At this moment Dionysus arises from the sea and consummates a love-marriage with her. Dionysus is the god not only of ecstasy, the *ecstasis* of the spirit as well as of wine and song, but he is also the god of death and the underworld. This divine visitant ravishes the soul of Ariadne. She thus experiences the transforming power of union with the dual aspects of intense life – the ecstatic life-giving spirit and the ecstasy of immersion in the instinctive stream of life that underlies and precedes conscious self-determination.

Maiuri suggests that the rite, pictured on the surrounding walls, portrays the initiation process as it was experienced by Roman women of classical times. The detailed description he gives, together with the many allusions to such rites and other corresponding materials, presents a coherent and convincing argument that these pictures are not concerned merely with a marriage rite or ceremony, as had formerly been suggested, but rather with the hidden ritual of initiation to the Orphic or Dionysiac mysteries which women of the century underwent in order to obtain transformation in this life, and probably as preparation for the next.

It is this material that Linda Fierz-David has undertaken to investigate from the psychological point of view in the present book. She discusses each of the pictured scenes in turn, using Professor Jung's analytic method to elucidate their psychological meaning. The result is a most impressive and convincing account of the stages of subjective development that women in antiquity passed through, guided by ritual happenings under the tutelage of older women who had themselves been initiated to the mysteries of the god. But beyond this, and of far greater importance for us today, she also shows by a detailed comparison with the individuation process that happenings similar to these can be, and are, experienced by modern women during the course of a deep introversion, usually undertaken under the guidance of an analyst.

The importance of such an understanding can hardly be overestimated in the present time, when, in revolt against the dogmatization of religion and culture, so many of our young people are plunging into the instinctual depths, not in order to find renewal, but in an autoerotic orgy that can only lead to the dissipation of life-energy and to a decadent and destructive primitivity. A far more serious and conscious attitude is needed if such a descent into primitive instinct is not to be merely destructive and chaotic. Union with the hidden instinctive forces, represented in the picture series in symbolic form as a phallic god, cannot be sought for personal satisfaction or aggrandizement without serious danger. These forces must be approached in a deeply religious spirit. The recognition that the ego is only a part of the total personality, and not even the most important part, is essential if the experience is to lead to life and not to death. The totality of the individual psyche is represented by an unknown and numinous factor which religions all over the world have always called god and which may only be approached in a spirit of humility. Arrogance or self-seeking may lead to a disastrous inflation, a danger graphically portrayed in the picture series almost as if it were a regular hazard on the initiation path.

Mrs. Fierz-David's discussion of the hidden and mysterious happenings represented by the pictures in the Villa makes this danger abundantly clear. Her description of what the emotional impact of the ritual must have been on the self-contained and dignified woman entering on the ritual way is most impressive and moving. One passes with this woman through the stages of her inner journey, as she listens first to the story of the marriage of Ariadne to the god, then begins step by step to relive in her own person Ariadne's experience: first the offering of herself, represented in the laurel twig she presents for consecration; then the descent to childhood, even to the animal level, so that she becomes a little kid, which, as the initiant declares, "falls into the milk." But as she is not a child, nor even a primitive, but a cultured and developed woman, even perhaps an intellectual one, she cannot be only a nursing kid; she must also be the little buck of the picture that represents the masculine part of the woman who has developed her mind and her ego-consciousness. He looks out into the room trying to hear and understand what the meaning of this strange metamorphosis of the woman might imply.

Up to this point, presumably, the stress of the initiation would be the same for a man as for a woman, although our picture series shows only a woman as initiant, possibly because this private sanctuary of the cult was reserved for women postulants. But now the paths of the man and the woman separate. After the experience of return to purely instinctive nature, the man must realize that in his totality he is no innocent lamb. For him to be immersed in natural instinct would inevitably lead also to identification with the negative and terrible, bestial side of man's animal nature, which is by no means only innocent and harmless. And so our pictures show the man as a young boy, forced to gaze into a bowl that reflects not his own face but a horrible demon-mask that is held up behind him. The boy sees this as his own countenance, implying that he experiences himself as identical with this aspect of masculinity that lurks in the unconscious background of every man. This scene takes place on the narrow back wall of the chamber which Mrs. Fierz-David suggests represents a sanctuary, sacred and secret, reserved for experiences in the immediate vicinity of the godhead.

A woman if she is truly womanly has a better chance of dealing with this aspect of the unconscious animal nature, for Mother Nature in her can face life, and death also, with compassion and relatedness. So, unless she is given over to the masculine side of her nature, she can confront such a manifestation without identifying with it. But a man cannot, as a rule, do this. For when he is confronted with an outburst of barbarism in others, he either tries to deal with it intellectually, with the principles of law and order and so on, or he falls into a correspondingly barbarous state in his attempts to master and eradicate the evil. This is an aspect of the psychological problem that Mrs. Fierz-David only indicates, since she is primarily concerned here with woman's psychology.

However, the woman of the picture series evidently saw the

possibility of this development and, terrified at the threatening aspect of the mask and realizing what such a descent into basic instinct might mean, she regains her human form and dashes right out of the picture, that is, out of the ritual situation and, as Mrs. Fierz-David suggests, plunges into the underground passage that actually exists in the Villa, where apparently the mystery of the god is revealed to her as phallus. But inasmuch as this is not represented as a sensuous man, intent on rape, but is a ritual object contained in the winnowing basket, traditionally the birth crib of the god, who is then reborn as a fertility daemon, the occurrence does not signify a sexual affair, but rather an inner happening that enables the woman to realize her own deepest sexual and erotic potentialities. In the pictured drama, however, she apparently does not fully understand the meaning of her visionary experience, for she emerges from the dark tunnel carrying the basket as if it were her own to do with as she wills. She is about to lift the veil that covers it when an angel swoops down to prevent the sacrilege.

In the psychological experience that corresponds to these pictured rituals, a modern woman, too, may become identified with her experience of the numinous, and it is not until she is chastised, not by an angry angelic visitant as in the pictured ritual, but by her own sense of guilt and her dismay at realizing the sacrilege she was about to commit, that she comes to her senses. The angel's name in the mysteries is evidence of this, for she is called Aidos, that is, modesty or humility, which would indeed be violated if the human woman claimed to be, in her own person, the elect, the chosen bride of the god of fertility, of instinct and of death. Such an attitude would result in an extreme of hybris, which would entirely de-humanize the actual woman, making her feel herself to be far above all common humanity as the bride of god.

As it is, she emerges again chastened and cleansed – born again, as a twice-born. And, interestingly enough, from here on she is no longer alone in the conscious dignity and self-possession of the first scene, but is received almost as a child into the company of initiated, that is, of mature women, now her sisters.

The self-contained, self-sufficient woman of the first scene has become one of the sisterhood of women who do not need to assert their value or themselves, either. Their value is obvious: they are among the wise ones, simple, natural, at one with themselves, whose inner dignity needs no advertisement; it is self-evident, as can be seen in the last picture of the series, thought to be a portrait of the Matrone, who surely represents the head and leader of the group of initiates who formed the core of the group of women whose headquarters were at this simple villa in Pompeii.

Mrs. Linda Fierz-David has done a remarkable piece of work that brings to life the world of the classical period and reveals it as not so very different from the world we know today. Her ability to pass from a description of the ritual depicted in the Villa to a psychological interpretation that is both valid and meaningful for modern women is one of the outstanding features of this fascinating study.

Her correlation of the ancient Roman world and culture with the modern situation throws a beam of light on the most pressing problems of woman's psychology in the present day. She gathers up the many classical allusions that illustrate the meaning of the frescoes themselves and shows how these same situations and problems confront the modern woman. The initiation depicted in the sequence of events in the mystery hall is to be met with by any woman during the process of individuation, and if she could understand the teachings represented by these cult pictures, she would be released from the sense of isolation and often of guilt that these experiences so often induce.

For the self-sufficient, outwardly well-adapted woman of today stands in need of initiation just as did her sister in the centuries immediately preceding the Christian era. Today there is no recognized mystery cult to which she can turn when the sterility of a merely adapted life overtakes her. (But then possibly the situation of the Villa, outside the city wall, also suggests that the cult was not officially recognized.) Consequently, the modern woman must walk a solitary path unless she can get help from psychological understanding. For the initiation today is necessarily a private and solitary affair taking place in the secret recesses of the heart. The analytical psychology of C. G. Jung, however, has made the secret transformations that can and do take place during an analytical experience available not only to those who undergo an analysis but also to the knowledge and understanding of all who study the wealth of material he has accumulated – provided they read with the heart as well as with the head.

Linda Fierz-David's insight into the deeper significance of these arresting and unique frescoes has given us not only a picture of the hidden meaning of the ancient mysteries of women but also a psychological interpretation of the steps that must be taken in the process. If we read with understanding, we too may embark on the road of inner self-confrontation that can bring us to the achievement of full maturity as women.

I personally am deeply indebted to her for the insight she has brought to this difficult and little-known subject, for it concerns a task that confronts all women of the twentieth century. This short introduction will, I hope, serve to whet the appetite of the reader, whom I will now refer to the competent guidance of our author.

M. Esther Harding
New York, 1966

Entering the Villa

History of the Villa of Mysteries

The Villa of Mysteries lies in a northerly direction outside of Pompeii, embedded in a gentle vineyard country. It shared the fate of Pompeii, a rich, little commercial town. Its famous wine that grew on the slopes of Vesuvius, along with other agricultural products, constituted a chief source of income. There were dye works, glass factories, and sauce factories where *garum* was made, a fermented fish sauce without which the Romans could not cook. Pompeii was visited by a terrible earthquake in 63 A.D. and was almost entirely destroyed. But no one paid attention to this warning from Heaven. The city was at once built up again in the most "modern" way. Its ruins are particularly instructive from a cultural-historical point of view, because it is a quintessence in miniature of the way of living of that time. It was this newly flourishing settlement that the great outbreak of Vesuvius in 79 A.D. destroyed. After the catastrophe only a wide field of ashes remained over the site of the city, and soon no one knew where Pompeii had been. Not until the year 1763, in the course of excavations that were still entirely unsystematic, was it realized that the ruins of the city had been come upon. And not until after the proclamation of the Kingdom of Italy in 1861 did careful investigation of the entire area of the city begin. Under this scholarly leadership an entire piece of the life of antiquity has been preserved and is accessible to us today.

The Villa of Mysteries, however, slept like an undisturbed Sleeping Beauty until 1910. Its discovery created an enormous sensation all over Europe, for there is hardly another excavation from classical times that can be compared with this jewel. I have myself experienced the impression that it makes. It was all the more amazing for me to visit, since I had already seen pictures of the Villa and its frescoes and read about them. But its reality was impressive in an entirely different way. I had looked first at the city of Pompeii and there, in spite of wandering through many interesting things, I had become melancholy. I do not know whether this was because the city included the ruins of so many new buildings, which had hardly been lived in, or because it was only a shopping city: everything seemed so soulless, and I felt cast down and empty. I then drove out to the Villa of Mysteries.

There I was completely shaken by the incredible interplay of noble simplicity and high culture, clear serenity and – I can only say – a truly numinous atmosphere. I was gripped by the deep shudder one feels in the face of a primitive experience. That this atmosphere is still preserved is evidence of the force of the psyche, for it was for only a relatively short time that the Villa housed a private Orphic cult, which served the initiation of aristocratic women. Even before the earthquake in 63 A.D., it was used as a private home; and after the earthquake, it was still employed as an agricultural factory. But no one seems to have dared do serious damage to the rooms in the front part of the house, which had religious significance. And the Initiation Chamber, with the frescoes about which I will speak, remained unchanged.

Amadeo Maiuri differentiates five building periods of the house, all of which I need not enumerate.[1] The first was a simple, square country-house of the third century B.C. that later became the foundation of a larger *villa rustica.* Maiuri says it underwent transformation from a country dwelling to a patrician, Roman city villa. This finally became – in the fourth building period (in Augustan times [31 B.C.–14 A.D.]) – the home of the private Orphic cult. The people who belonged to the cult must also have lived there – some perhaps only temporarily, others perhaps permanently. This can be ascertained from the great number of living rooms and sleeping cells of Roman style. The roomy *triclinium* (a "three couch" dining room) also leads one to think that the Villa must have served a large group of people. Many rooms and sleeping cells were painted, partly with Pompeiian designs, partly with very lively pictures of figures, some of which also mirrored life in the Villa. They must have had an extraordinarily gay, colorful, and charming effect. The Villa possessed a large and a small *atrium* (courts open to the sky), the latter entirely lost today except to the eye of the dreamer. In back of this smaller *atrium* lay a roomy *peristyle*, an enclosed inner court surrounded by pillars. It in turn was surrounded by terraces and colonnades.

In comparison with the Villa's charming building style, civilized conveniences were very modest. In the cooking courtyard, to be sure, there was a *hypocaust* (a subterranean furnace for heating water) for a comparatively small bathing arrangement and a bake-oven; but there were no heating and no plumbing, as was customary for the houses of the better classes. Perhaps one might call living in the Villa puritanical in the old Roman style – with only the lasting things of the culture present without the ephemeral padding of civilization. Today, when we are so fascinated by civilized standards, we can hardly measure the great understanding of life expressed by this simplicity. For modern parallels, we might turn to Weimar, or the Schloss Tiefurt of the Duchess Amalie, or also, in miniature, Goethe's Garden House on the Stern. (It is possible that Shakespeare's house in Stratford-on-Avon has a similar significance.) There, too, the fullness of the culture makes its impact, and there, too, civilized comforts are absent. In these places, it is spiritual values alone that speak through things. It is in this way that we must think of the Villa of Mysteries.

Despite inconvenience, life in the Villa must have been happy. For example, there are remnants of a mural where certain ladies are feasting together most comfortably, and there are other paintings with very gay Dionysian scenes. Yet life in the Villa cannot have been orgiastic. This we can determine with the greatest assurance. For the keynote of the Villa of Mysteries was a portrait-like statue of the Empress Livia, which was found in the *peristyle* in 1929. Since the main entrance of the Villa led from the back of the house directly into the *peristyle* (in a manner not altogether usual), this statue was the first thing that met the eyes of the arriving visitor.

Livia, the wife of the Emperor Augustus (57 B.C.–29 A.D.), signified for the entire Roman world of that time a cultural conviction and a political program. Livia was the first representative of what we would today call the conservative nobility. She stood against the impinging Orientalism which had ruined Marcus Antonius and which later ruined Caligula and Nero, the last ruler of the Claudian imperial family. She represented the Roman tradition and the European values developed in Rome, which attained their fullness after the Greek inheritance had been absorbed by Rome. This had already happened by the last centuries of the Republic. In Livia's time, for example, elementary children were already bilingual. In the Augustan time, however – even in Caesar's time (100 to 44 B.C.) – the Roman and the Greek spirit were recognized as the *united European spirituality*. Virgil, who was entirely a Roman and entirely an heir of Greece, is almost a legend because he served the coming to consciousness of this meaningful *conjunctio*. The same cultural meaning was carried on the feminine side by Livia. Not Greece but *Rome,* and indeed already at the time of the Republic, was the birthplace of the European woman as a product of culture and bearer of culture. Even though customs were far from ours now, the Roman woman was educated and also emancipated, in the same sense we understand these terms today. And this was true not only of married women. The Romans were such skillful lawyers that, in spite of the laws, they placed unmarried women on an equal basis with matrons. As Guglielmo Ferrero said in his book *The Women of the Caesars,* placing women on an equal basis with men, which we so gladly claim as our own high moral aim, was first reached by women in Rome.[2]

Livia, as woman, at the side of the Emperor Augustus, could truly represent European spirituality and morality. Her husband – with all his charm, enjoyment of life, and subtlety – was a plebeian; but she brought him into her culture of the nobility, for she, the Claudian, was sprung from the oldest nobility. The Casa Augustea, where the imperial pair lived as rulers for over forty years, was Livia's creation and mirrored her culture. This modest little palace was kept unchanged after the death of the couple and is still shown to marveling generations as a shining example – as in modern times marveling generations visit Weimar.

All her life, under very difficult circumstances, Livia served the Emperor Augustus – and with him, the state. She did so with steadfast loyalty, with an almost mute discretion, and – when she had to – with feminine ill temper too. She had behind her not only the wide circle of the nobility, but also the people. When Augustus was dead she, together with her like-minded daughter-in-law Antonia, became a power in support of the state in the midst of the often convulsive uncertainties of the Claudian government. Even during her lifetime Livia became a symbol or rather, perhaps, a *type*. Augustus himself had consciously presented her in this sense.

This image of woman represented by Livia has never been lost to Western countries. In regard to worldly forms of life, Christendom has indeed remained indebted to the Roman pattern. This is especially true for women. The outstanding women of the Middle Ages followed the type of Livia, insofar as they could attain effectiveness in the world. One example was Markgräfin Mathelda von Toscana, who played so great a role in the struggle between the emperor and the pope and whom Dante reverently placed in the earthly Paradise next to Beatrice. In the Renaissance the type of Livia came strongly to life again and acted – I might almost say – as an *archetypal* symbol for the educated, progressive woman of the times. Goethe too had an inkling of this symbol. His *Iphigenia,* which, indeed, he wrote in Italy, is not to be thought of without the highly cultivated Roman concept of the woman in whom tranquility, tact, and active decisiveness are united. And when Goethe writes in *Tasso,*

> Willst Du erfahren, was sich ziemt,
> so frage nur bei edeln Frauen an. . . .
>
> Wilt thou know what is seemly,
> just ask among highborn women. . . .

the image that we may call Livia stands behind it.

The image embodied by Livia is for us somewhat incomplete because the conscious, ethical formulation of motherhood was lacking in the Roman woman. This was first developed by the Christian world. The ideal of the Mother Mary first taught women to cultivate their motherliness and to make its feeling value conscious. Of course Roman women could be good mothers too, but motherliness in them remained in thrall to nature and was always subordinated to social and political necessities. In the Roman woman the relationship *to the man* became conscious and cultivated. I would put it in this order: first was her relationship to the father, to whom the woman owed her education, freedom, and also the traditional forms of her piety; second, her relationship to the preceptor, whom the girl of the better classes had after the elementary school (which she attended along with the boys) up to the time of her marriage, and who could be both teacher and friend;[3] and third, her relationship to the men whose companion and fellow worker she was and whose dangerous fate she often shared in all its severity in the time of the Empire.

Until now I have spoken of Livia alone, but even a woman like Livia could not have become a prototype in this way if so many nameless women of the nobility had not formed a foundation for her, devoting themselves to this courageous empress and striving to be like her. Like Livia, countless cultivated women of Rome suffered under the terrible spiritual and intellectual conflicts into which the conquered Orient dragged the victor. I cannot here go into the shocking tragedy which these conflicts meant for these women of the Julian-Claudian Imperial House. They were tragic for all women of that time, whose feeling for European values was awake and alive.

It is such women, who fought and suffered like Livia, who we must think of as participants in the cult of the Villa of Mysteries. They must have been women sufficiently wellborn to have dared to erect a statue of the Empress Livia and to gather around it, well-educated enough to sense the difficulty of imperial problems, alive enough to sense that the life of a woman is not fulfilled, even when the relationship to the fathers, and to male teachers and companions, is lived.

This very brief picture, which is only an introduction, naturally leaves many questions unanswered. Later we will discuss in detail the frescoes of the Initiation Chamber of the Villa of Mysteries. What I would particularly like to emphasize here is that we can feel sympathy with these Roman women. Those women who sought fulfillment in the cult of the Villa were not so different that we cannot understand them and learn from them. Indeed, it is still through the Roman "pattern" that the modern woman seeks to realize her emancipation. Already in the second century B.C., a Roman prototype of the modern woman's association existed in the very influential *conventus matronarum,* a ladies' club, and also in women's gatherings and women's demonstrations. In Roman times too, it was precisely the intelligent women who were afflicted with the distressing feeling that the world cannot solve all problems. We shall speak about the differences that exist between Roman women and our modern selves in due time, for they too can be instructive.

Naturally Livia had her opponents and antagonists also. The most important and dangerous – for the state as well as for Livia – was the older Julia (born 39 B.C.), the daughter of Augustus by his first marriage. This Julia was Livia's truly opposite pole, for she represented the "modern," cosmopolitan outlook on the world, which wished without reservation to take possession of the abundant possibilities of the Empire and savor them completely. This was an understandable urge, for Rome had to absorb the spiritual as well as material goods of conquered peoples. It was at the same time a terrible instrument of moral corruption, as one can see in the example of Julia. This beloved child of Augustus must have been a gorgeous young woman. She had inherited love of life and loveableness from her father: certainly she had more charm than Livia. All hearts went out to her; she gathered about her a large group of cosmopolitans who wished not only to rule but enjoy, who claimed not only all the riches of the cultures opened up by Rome, but also all the finesse of international civilization. Julia and her adherents became a power in the state, and for many years Livia was wise enough to grant her stepdaughter all the power she wanted.

In the year 21 B.C., Julia was united in a second marriage with Augustus's most loyal comrade-in-arms, Agrippa, who in 18 B.C. was designated co-regent of the Emperor. Therefore Julia became equal to her stepmother. With her aging spouse Agrippa, she then made a triumphant Oriental journey around the world, during which she allowed herself to be deified as Aphrodite on the Greek islands. Here we see the moral corruption: Julia, head of the "modern" party, *was the first* to introduce into the Roman Imperial family the idea of apotheosis during one's lifetime – an idea very foreign to the Roman spirit. *She* was the model for a Caligula or Nero, a historical fact that one dare not overlook, especially if one wishes to understand correctly the significance of Livia.

Livia did not thwart Julia for as long as she could possibly help it. Yet Livia was the only one who dared take action against the darling child of Augustus, when Julia's party became a real danger to the state. In the year 2 B.C., when she finally did overthrow her step-daughter and drive her into lifelong banishment, it was with a cold premeditation that could seem inhuman. The Empress acted then with the greatest decisiveness, and she had a super-personal right on her side. She was standing, as she would again and again, for her native soil and for the *inheritance of the ancestors,* who are our forebears also. What Virgil, the writer of the *Georgics,* represented as poet, Livia represented by living, acting, and suffering – namely, for love of homeland in the midst of the tumult of imperial development. Therefore Livia is great, even though she had plenty of shadow sides. And the circle of women who assembled about her had on their side also the greatest developmental possibilities – that is, those of the future.

The Initiation Chamber

If one goes from the entrance of the Villa, through the *peristyle* and the large *atrium,* one finds the Initiation Chamber in the front half of the house on the left side. The room is 7 by 5 meters (about 23 by 16 feet), with a black-and-white mosaic floor. In the middle of the long wall on the east is a large window which looks out on a covered terrace. Likewise along the southwestern short wall, a wide door leads to a covered terrace, from which the view of the gently sloping plain was probably very pretty. One reaches the entrance to the chamber from the interior of the house through two cells which open into one another. The first is presumed to have served as a cloakroom. In the second, sacrifices appear to have been made. Remains of small bones have been found and, in a wall cabinet, sacrificial vessels. At this point, a small entrance door was broken through the wall into the chamber. Starting at this entrance door, the frescoes go around the room between an upper and a lower frieze. They contain a total of 29 human figures, which impress one as almost life-size. The upright figures measure 145-155 cm. in height (about 57-61 inches). The frescoes are divided into scenes, whose

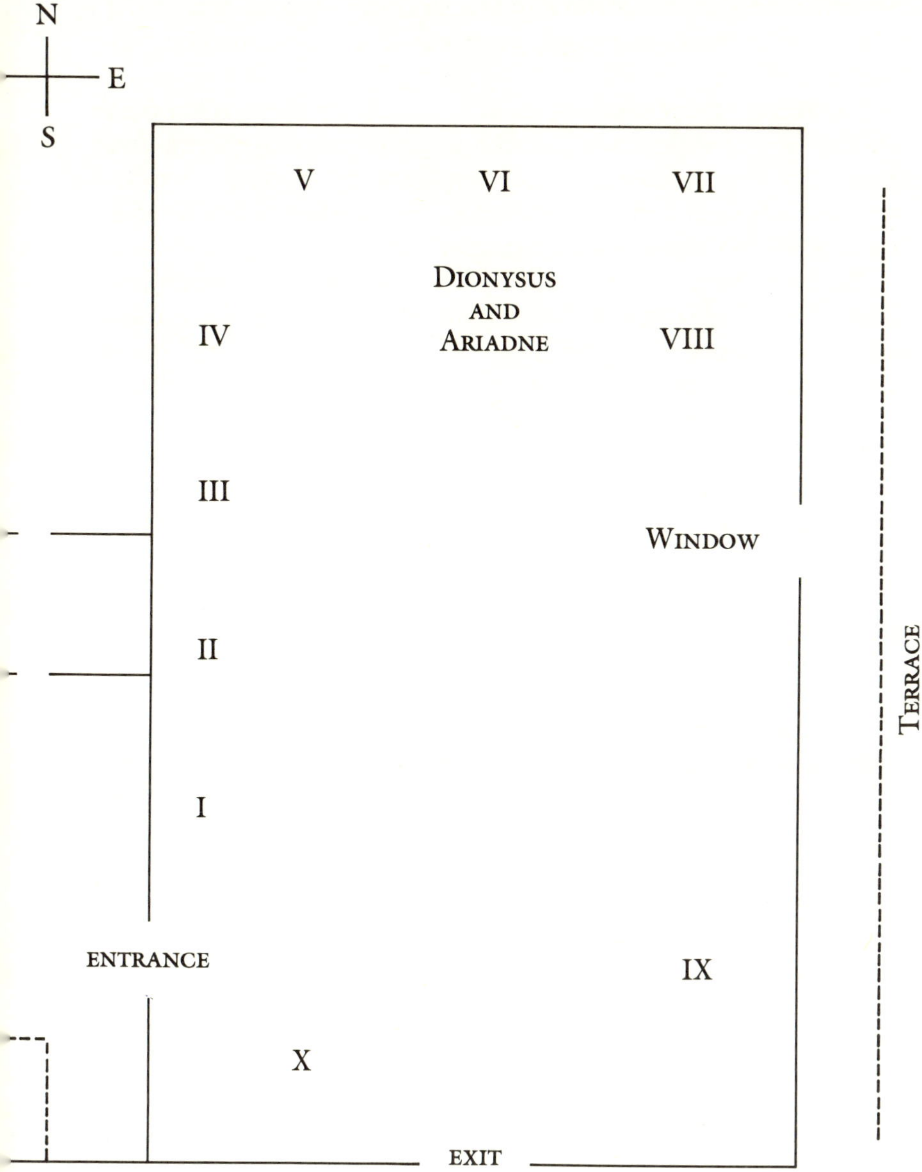
N
E
S
V
VI
VII
Dionysus
and
Ariadne
IV
VIII
III
Window
II
Terrace
I
ENTRANCE
IX
X
EXIT

order I shall give as recorded by Maiuri. I will describe them briefly below, so we can get a quick overview of the plan and discuss its significance.

The First Scene on the long inner wall close to the small entrance shows the veiled figure of a listening initiate whose gestures surely have ritual significance. A naked boy reads to her from a scroll. A priestess who sits behind him directs him in doing so and, at the same time, looks attentively at the initiate.

The Second Scene is introduced by the figure of a woman, crowned with myrtle, who carries a cake. She brings it to an altar table at which a priestess is just beginning to carry out a ritual act. To the left of the priestess, a serving woman holds a covered basket. To her right a young priestess pours out water for a libation.

The Third Scene is introduced by the figure of a half-naked Silenus, who is playing the lyre. Next to him, by a small group of rocks, sit a young faun and a panisk (a female pan figure). A little kid presses close to the faun, who plays the flute; a second kid sucks at the breast of the panisk. In the very front stands a young buck listening attentively.

The Fourth Scene contains only a single figure – the so-called terrified woman, who throws on her cloak and appears to flee.

The long inner wall ends here.

In *the Fifth Scene,* on the back wall of the chamber, we see at first a seated Silenus, who seems to turn his attention back to the terrified woman. At the same time, he lifts a metal vessel to his other side. A young faun behind him bends and gazes into the vessel. Behind this faun stands a second young faun who smilingly raises a Dionysian mask of terror.

The Sixth Scene, in the middle of the back wall, is unfortunately greatly damaged. It shows the commanding picture of Dionysus, who leans against his beloved Ariadne. A beribboned *thyrsus* (staff) lies across his knees.

In *the Seventh Scene* we first see the figure of a kneeling woman with a cap. Her features are distorted, eyes widely staring. She carries a torch over her shoulder; before her stands the *liknon,* the Bacchic winnowing basket. Her gesture looks as if she were just trying to raise the cover from a great phallus within it. Behind her, only just visible, are two highly agitated figures of women. In front of her hovers a black-winged angel raising its hand against her, to ward her off. At the same time, with the other hand, which carries a whip, the angel lifts its arm for a blow. This scene is usually designated as the *Flagellation*. Here the back wall of the chamber ends, and for this reason Maiuri reckons the next figure as . . .

The Eighth Scene. Here kneels the half-naked figure of a despairing woman, filled with terror, for it is she at whom the blow of the angel is aimed. She has laid her head in the lap of the woman sitting by her, who gazes at the angel. The next figure in this scene is a very erect, naked Bacchante who turns her back to the viewer. A beautifully dressed woman who carries the *thyrsus* seems to dance around her. This scene takes up the space along the long outer wall up to the window.

On the other side of the window, *the Ninth Scene* shows a lady whose hair is being dressed by her maid. An Erotes (a cupid figure) holds the mirror for her while a second Erotes, on the other side of the lady, looks placidly on.

Here the long outer wall comes to an end.

Along the short outer wall, on the other side of the large exit door which leads to the terrace in front of the house, there is only one scene, *the Tenth Scene:* it portrays a richly dressed lady who rests in a reclining chair and leans one arm on a cushion. This picture is often designated as *The Domina* because it is believed to be the portrait of the Lady of the House.

That this series of pictures belonged to a private Orphic cult is generally supposed. Maiuri is of this opinion and has compiled evidence to justify this conclusion. He also reasons that the companion of Dionysus in the large central panel is Ariadne. Most scholars agree on these two points. But they do not agree on anything else; on the contrary, the most varied conjectures have led to the most violent controversies, at least for now. For this reason, many modern scholars content themselves with the declaration that nothing can be known about the meaning of the frescoes. It is true that the Villa itself gives us no information: it contains no word, no inscription, that might refer to the cult. It is a *casa muta* that, in this respect, might perhaps be compared with the well-known alchemical text the *Liber Mutus*.

Stimulated by the German research worker Margarete Bieber, the opinion first prevailed that the frescoes were concerned, at least in part, with the initiation rites of a bride before her wedding.[4] This German researcher is often and eagerly cited, for her proposal would decidedly have been the easiest solution. The representation of Dionysus and Ariadne would, in that case, be conceived as the prototype of marriage. The scene of the flagellation is compared with fertility rites as they occurred, for example, in Sparta in the Temple of Artemis Orthia or in the Roman Lupercalia, where girls were lashed with a whip in order to make them fertile.

A naive soul can probably be satisfied with that kind of interpretation. But it cannot be right, if only for this reason: Roman girls were usually married for the first time very young, mostly between the twelfth and sixteenth years.[5] This, and the fact that marriages were so easily dissolved and that many women married several times, is the greatest difference between the life of the Roman and the modern woman. The women on the frescoes of the Villa are not children, and the terrible scene with the black-winged angel and the despairing, kneeling woman cannot be compared with the carnival usages of Lupercalia. This is entirely apart from the fact that the union of Dionysus and Ariadne does not refer to an earthly wedding, but to the full depth of meaning of a transformation mystery.

We must, therefore, start with the fact that there is no tradition for the frescoes of the Villa of Mysteries that we can depend upon. But these pictures have something so unusually lively and original – they so clearly represent the experience of development from a beginning stage to a goal – that I asked myself whether one might not regard them from a psychological standpoint, like a dream series, for example, and methodically amplify the separate symbols. The conscious situation of the Roman woman at the beginning of the Empire, as I pointed out earlier, is known in general and we can feel empathy with it. This empathy is necessary for a psychological approach. (One hypothesis necessary for such a way of thinking would indeed be met by this fact.) We can also fall back upon richly flowing sources of pertinent mythological material. I call attention here provisionally only to S. Roscher's *Lexikon der griechischen-römischen Mythologie,* Walter F. Otto's *Dionysus,* Erwin Rohde's *Psyche,* and Professor Kerényi's *The Gods of the Greeks.* I have also had the good fortune to hear Professor Kerényi's lectures to a private circle in Zürich.[5a] I also consulted with him personally, and he holds, as I do, that it is permissible to draw upon the most varied versions and traditions of the Dionysus myths for aid in understanding. The frescoes of the Villa certainly stem from a time when all myths already flowed together in the great mixing bowl of Hellenism.

The psychological hypothesis follows directly from the plan of the fresco series. This plan follows a distinguishing pattern: the pictures run in a circle around the hall, but not one of the figures of the pictures is turned toward the great central picture of Dionysus and Ariadne. Not one figure looks directly at this couple, and those that stand closest are expressly turned away. Also, the two figures of Dionysus and Ariadne themselves are not related at all to the other figures; they are complete in themselves. This is so noticeable that one must consider it first of all. Dionysus and Ariadne are indeed the center of the whole picture-history; one could therefore imagine a representation of them also in the middle of the hall. But they stand independent and for themselves, inaccessible to everything else. One might even say they are represented as *being there invisibly.* They personify the central symbol that is removed from human eyes, that unites the ancient opposites of the masculine and the feminine in the *conjunctio*. Psychologically expressed, this means that in this room Dionysus-Ariadne is the symbol of the Self.

With this center, the room as a whole forms a great mandala. It, in turn, is made of many small mandalas, since every one of the other scenes contains a symbol which corresponds to the central symbol and, in a way, stands in its stead. When one has slipped through the narrow entrance door – and this slipping through is already the first symbol of initiation – one stands in a *temenos*, a consecrated circle; and in walking through the chamber from one of the small mandalas to another, one performs a *circumambulatio,* which, leading toward a goal, constantly unfolds new meaning. These patterns point clearly to individuation symbolism. Psychologically, the arrangement in the chamber might represent the individuation process. The cyclical or spiral way around a governing center that from step to step manifests itself in changing forms, but itself always remains hidden – this is chiefly what we understand as the individuation process.

As C. G. Jung states:

> The way to the goal seems chaotic and interminable at first, and only gradually do the signs increase that it is leading anywhere. The way is not straight but appears to go round in circles. More accurate knowledge has proved it to go in spirals: the dream-motifs always return after certain intervals to definite forms, whose characteristic it is to define a centre. . . . We might draw a parallel between such spiral courses and the processes of growth in plants; in fact the plant motif (tree, flower, etc.) frequently recurs in these dreams and fantasies and is also spontaneously drawn or painted. In alchemy the tree is the symbol of Hermetic philosophy.[6]

(The corresponding symbol of our Orphic mystery cult is, as will be demonstrated in the seventh fresco scene, Dionysus as a spruce tree.)

> The development of these symbols is almost the equivalent of a healing process. The centre or goal thus signifies *salvation* in the proper sense of the word. . . . It seems to me beyond all doubt that these processes are concerned with the religion-creating archetypes. Whatever else religion may be, those psychic ingredients of it which are empirically verifiable undoubtedly consist of unconscious manifestations of this kind.[7]

Of course we must apprehend the idea of this process broadly enough – and enough in terms of universal humanity – if we wish to make use of it for an ancient initiation mystery. For that purpose, I can best refer to a place from Jung's *Psychology and Alchemy,* which contains a comprehensive statement of the individuation process upon which we shall depend throughout:

> Natural man is not a "self" – he is the mass and a particle in the mass, collective to such a degree that he is not even sure of his own ego. That is why since time immemorial he has needed the transformation mysteries to turn

him into something, and to rescue him from the animal collective psyche, which is nothing but a *variété*.

But if we reject this unseemly *variété* of man "as he is," it is impossible for him to attain integration, to become a self. And that amounts to spiritual death. Life that just happens in and for itself is not real life; it is real only when it is *known*. Only a unified personality can experience life, not that personality which is split up into partial aspects, that bundle of odds and ends which also calls itself "man."[8]

These are entirely general but nevertheless impressive formulations of the problem of individuation, or becoming a self. This process leads from the fundamental insecurity of natural man, ensnared in the world, through a complete transformation into a unified, liberated personality. The people of ancient times who experienced this transformation in the mystery cults were also driven by the necessity to escape spiritual death. We must know life, as Jung says, but the people of ancient times learned this in a somewhat different manner than we: they learned *by submitting themselves* to the sacred happening of a cult drama, as it was handed down by tradition, in order to repeat the experience of divine fate and divine transformation.

As long as the old myths were alive for mankind, participation in a mystery cult could be an original experience for each individual; that is, through a cult, the participant could be directly touched through archetypal images, could be deeply affected by them, and thus could be rescued from the animal, collective psyche which is nothing but a hodgepodge (*variété*). However, from the frescoes of the Villa, it seems this hodgepodge was not rejected by the Orphic cult.

I have stated this in so much detail because it is important to be clear about our point of departure. My hypothesis is that the frescoes of the Villa of Mysteries portray individuation processes in a form suitable to our time. It is merely a working hypothesis, and it is still to be shown how far it proves to be right. It will all depend upon whether the ideas we may form with the help of this hypothesis are clear, whether they hang together, and whether we succeed again and again in picking out the thread that guides us from step to step and reveals meaning compatible with a process.

If I express myself more personally than is customary here in the following material, please forgive me and do not ascribe it to immodesty. I must not conceal it when my reflections have been suggested by individual impressions. Anyway, concern about this would be unnecessary since the psychological standpoint of Jungian doctrine, upon which I depend throughout, guarantees scientific objectivity.

It is also purely from this standpoint that I use the inestimably rich materials which research in old philologies has given us. We owe it to this research that psychological reflections such as the following are at all possible today. This obliges me, of course, never to overstep the boundaries of analytical psychology. Therefore, I will go as little as possible into the controversies over the meaning of the fresco series in the Villa of Mysteries which has occupied classical scholars. These will only find mention insofar as seems necessary for psychological analysis.

The Mythological Hypothesis of the Mystery Cult: Dionysus and Ariadne

In order to be clear, we must include some introductory notes on the meaning of the central picture in the Initiation Hall. These comments are not intended to state anything exhaustive about the great figures of Dionysus and Ariadne. We dare not anticipate their full significance. It is part of the meaning of the mystery cult that the divine reality of these two dominant figures reveals itself step by step in the course of the initiation ceremony in a way that suits the participant's capacity to experience each moment. In every single scene of the frescoes, therefore, we meet first Dionysus and then Ariadne again and again in a new manner. We shall learn to understand their meaning as we observe how the participant in the mystery came to know them. What I must try to convey in the following paragraphs is, therefore, merely a hint that Dionysus and Ariadne are indeed symbols of a central character; psychologically speaking, they personify the Self and becoming a Self.

In the Orphic cult it is Dionysus's fate that the participant in the mystery relives. It is possible that the prominence of this godlike-demonic figure has caused certain modern researchers to pretend to be naive in relation to the meaning of the frescoes and to maintain that it was only a preparation for a wedding. The fear of early Christendom which saw in Dionysus the diabolical rival of Christ, and also the fear of the Middle Ages which saw him as the king of the witches, continues to echo today.[9] (When we think of the fate of Nietzsche, we can perhaps understand this.) The old Thracian Dionysus was a sinister figure – ruler of the dead and of souls, who stormed through the forests with the legendary Maenads and bore his devotees violently away into orgies, but who also lent them the gift of prophecy. This first connection with the infernal regions was present in all formulations of the Dionysus figure. Even in Delphi, where Dionysus is reconciled with Apollo, he is the sun of the dark wintertime – an underworld sun, one might say – and even there he was worshiped with frenzy. Heraclitus says of Dionysus, "It is Hades for whom they rave and celebrate feasts";[10] that is, death is in the air near Dionysus. He is the wild huntsman, but also the hunted wild creature; he is the devourer (*omēstēs* – the eater) and also the one who is devoured. He strikes people with madness, but as Dionysus Lysios he also delivers them from delusion. Dismembered and reborn, he is a typical savior-god.

According to Orphic tradition, he is the son of the chthonic Zeus in the form of a snake and of Persephone, and as such is called Dionysus-Zagreus. Jealous Hera incites the Titans against the young huntsman, and it is said that during his flight from them he takes on the forms of animals: he becomes a kid, a deer, and a bull. The Titans nevertheless overtake him, tear him apart, and eat the pieces. Only his heart is saved by Pallas Athene; she brings it to Father Zeus. Zeus shatters the guilty Titans with his lightning-bolt, and they burn to ashes. From these ashes, however, according to Orphic tradition, human beings originate; and this is the Orphic teaching – that human beings have thereby inherited the nature of the Titans and their guilt.

In this Greek tradition, therefore, an inherited guilt is the parallel of the Christian original sin. With the guilt, however, all human beings have also inherited, in the ashes of the Titans, a particle of the god whom they had devoured. Since then, human beings are torn by the conflict raging within them between their Titan nature and the divine part which is their immortal soul. The Orphic mystery cult seeks to atone for the Titan guilt and to free humans from their conflict, as they ceremonially relive the fate of the god. If the humans die in the mystery ceremonial, as the god did, their divine spark is freed and unites itself with the god.

There are two traditions about the rebirth of the god. According to one, Zeus hid the heart of Zagreus in his thigh and brought him into the world again himself. According to the other, he gave the heart to his earthly love, Semele, in a drink. As she bore the new Dionysus, Zeus killed her with his lightning-bolt. In this connection, Kerényi once spoke of Dionysus as thrice-born (born once of Zagreus, once from the thigh of Zeus, and once of Semele).

The two versions of the rebirth seem to indicate something like a dilemma in relation to the creative process which was evident at that time all over the Mediterranean area. There appeared everywhere at that time the image of the dying and self-renewing Savior, but in the Greek area the symbol of the renewal was especially ambiguous. If Dionysus was reborn from the thigh of Zeus, then the process takes place entirely on the other side, in the realm of the gods, removed from mankind, and the one who is reborn is a god *only.* If, on the other hand, Zeus hands the dangerous sacred drink to a woman, then the human element is added and Dionysus lives again as a god-man. Then, for the first time, there is a true parallel with Christ.

In general this latter version has prevailed. In this case Semele, the mother of the god-man, remains a pure figure, like the mother of Christ, since Zeus removed her from the earth through his fire during the act of birth (which did not proceed from sexual union but from a drink). She lives on then, in the underworld, until Dionysus redeems her and brings her to the celestial sphere. In the same manner he also redeems the Bacchantes who died for him. Many legends about martyrs are connected with his cult. All these are also prototypes for Orphic initiation; in them Dionysus appears always as redeemer.

The one who arises again is then the triumphant Dionysus, who becomes more and more a symbol of unification. He is not only the god-man whose cyclical appearance is celebrated on earth; as ruler of souls he remains a Hades. He is life and death in one. He is not only fiery and inflaming, he is also watery, for he always comes out of the water – out of a sea or over the ocean. As kid, as bull, he is animal; in ivy, in wine, in pine and spruce, he is plant-like. He is the small child, the handsome lad, *and* the mature, bearded man. After his rebirth in the winnowing basket or in the Orphic fruit basket, he appears as phallus, that is, as the creative principle. The *human* Dionysus figure, however, has never been portrayed as a phallus. Here, through the interweaving of masculine and feminine features, it is indicated that he is hermaphrodite – masculine and feminine – intellect and soul in one.

Finally, the Orphic Dionysus embodies the Self as the center of psychic life, in that he unites in himself all opposites (in this connection, see the text for the fresco scenes further on) and at the same time becomes for mankind a redeeming image of the goal. Nevertheless, this center of psychic life does not manifest itself in Dionysus as a heavenly light or as a higher order. *Dionysus always shines forth from the depths.* He is always the entirely unexpected, that which overtakes one, shuddering; an irrational, emotional event that wells up; a shock that befalls from which one cannot withdraw. But Dionysus is still more: for that which always remains alive with him, that which never dies, and that from which the renewal results, is his heart. In its deepest sense, that is the essence of Dionysus: beating heart, loving glow. Consequently, where Dionysus appears as symbol of the Self, there in the center stands the heart and, with it, a whole gamut of feelings: from the bittersweet of heart-rending passion, to the deadly peril of love, to rejoicing with and having sympathy for all living creatures, and to the strange feeling of new highest values through which the human heart and human depths can be seized, transformed, and redeemed.

But the whole meaning of Dionysus and our mystery cult arises from his union with Ariadne. Kerényi once said there is in Greek mythology no other couple that can be compared with Dionysus and Ariadne. And truly, in this one couple the masculine and the feminine, the divine and the human, pervade one another completely and are thereby transformed.

Ariadne was a daughter of the mythical Cretan King Minos and of

Pasiphaë. Here we find ourselves on an entirely archaic, chthonic level. The chthonic Zeus as a bull and Europa were the parents of Minos and his brothers, who were therefore sons of a bull. The parents of Pasiphaë were Helios, the old Sun, and Perseïs, a figure that is also connected with the sun. In the daughter Pasiphaë, the primeval light of the parents changes over into darkness; she is a heavenly cow of the night, and she appears therefore in myths as spouse of the son of the bull. As children of gods, Minos and Pasiphaë are divine; as mythical king and queen, they are human.

Minos and Pasiphaë have certain difficulties before they can produce human children. Minos at first produces only swarming insects instead of semen; he was first freed from this evil by the loving Procris (who gave him a prophylactic drink concocted by the witch Circe – the drink prevented his filling her with reptiles and insects). Pasiphaë, on the other hand, at first prefers a vagabond sun-bull, of whom the myth tells nothing more, and through him she becomes the mother of the frightful Minotaur. (In order to hide him, the artist Daedalus built the famous Cretan labyrinth, a subterranean mandala.) Only later do the two human daughters of these parents, Ariadne and Phaidra, come into the world.

We have here an example of what many term the *chronique scandaleuse* of Greek mythology. Actually, this myth is concerned with a meaningful symbolic representation of an entirely unconscious primeval situation. Symbolically, mythical Crete is a chthonic paradise where the spiritual, masculine principle appears at first merely as pricking excitement and the feeling, feminine principle only as vagabond instinctuality. All forces rule here – the divine and the animal, the life-bestowing and the life-destroying – and they are as undifferentiated as they are holy.

In this primeval area, opposites clearly diverge for the first time in Ariadne and Phaidra. Ariadne, or Ariagne, is a human-divine girl; she is mortal, but carries the important surname of Persephone – the untouchably pure, the most holy. This name indicates that Ariadne has a dark, underworld character; therefore, she also knows the way into the underworld labyrinth. Phaidra, on the other hand, is the shining, bright one; she belongs entirely to the world of day, and in her the human prevails.

The myth tells how Ariadne falls into sin. It tells that she belonged to the bull-god Dionysus, but becomes untrue to him when she falls in love with the Athenian Theseus and helps him kill her half-brother, the Minotaur, in order to put an end to the annual human sacrifice which he demands. Then she (together with Phaidra) flees from Crete with Theseus, who promises Ariadne marriage. Theseus is a figure of light, a sun hero; and, at the same time, as an Athenian, he evokes the idea of human culture. By fleeing with him, Ariadne turns her back on her own dark origin. But during the homeward journey, without having consummated their marriage, Theseus deserts Ariadne on the island of Naxos while she sleeps. (This idea of the deserted, sleeping Ariadne on Naxos has become a favorite theme in art.)

According to one tradition, it is Artemis who sends Theseus away from Naxos at the wish of the enraged Dionysus and who kills Ariadne there. Theseus then takes Phaidra with him to Athens as his spouse. According to another version, Ariadne hangs herself in despair on Naxos. Then, however, there is a grand turning point in the dramatic action. Dionysus, coming from the sea, approaches the island and consummates a holy marriage with Ariadne. In the beginning of his drama *Ariadne on Naxos,* Hofmannsthal represents the turning from despair to fulfillment with extraordinary meaning. The forsaken Ariadne is alone, she calls out, she longs for death, and as Dionysus approaches, she does not recognize him. It is *death* into whose arms she casts herself. And Dionysus does not recognize Ariadne either. He, the bringer of madness, is himself out of his senses; he too calls out, he longs for his mother, and he finds Ariadne. This representation is mythologically true, for Ariadne is secretly, in mortal form, indeed the untouchably pure Persephone, the earliest mother of Dionysus. Here he embraces her as his beloved. And as for Ariadne, the underworld ruler of souls is death, who, however, brings her transformation and resurrection through the holy marriage. In this connection, Ariadne on Naxos is also named Aridela. The word *aridelos* means "very clear, clearly visible." This, therefore, means that Ariadne, who was previously a dark figure, becomes clarified on Naxos.

But Dionysus too is transformed there, for on Naxos he discovers wine. The bull-god thus becomes the god of wine. There is a very lovely Roman relief which shows Dionysus resting on Naxos, as he holds Ariadne on his knees. With one arm he pushes forward a small, earnest old Silenus, who presents the first vessel of wine.[11] According to Roman texts, after the wedding Dionysus carries Ariadne in his wagon up to Heaven. This is the liveliest classical version of an ascension. The best known tradition, however, is that, in remembrance of Ariadne, Dionysus sets among the stars the golden crown of Aphrodite, which he had previously given Ariadne.

Ariadne's way is a mythical representation of the transformation process that we today call the individuation process. She lives at first in the realm of Minos and Pasiphaë, in paradisaic unconsciousness where all things – God, human and animal – are undifferentiated. Here too there is as yet no guilt, since Pasiphaë remains unchanged and guiltless even when she bears the Minotaur. With Theseus, the light of consciousness dawns. Ariadne turns toward him, and with him a penetration into the labyrinth of earthiness becomes possible, a coming to terms with the blind, destructive instincts represented by the Minotaur. Thus Ariadne loses contact with the light that is concealed in the earth and has always ruled her, represented here by Dionysus who, as bull, embodies the creative fire of the emotions. In fleeing with Theseus, Ariadne gives herself over entirely to the principle of consciousness and disavows the darkness of her origin: the unconscious and the soul are suppressed. She hurries beyond herself toward the light of the world (Athens) in order to be one-sidedly conscious.

But Ariadne is crossed by Artemis. This surely means that the feminine, moon-like principle, that indeed rules in every woman, does not endure the one-sidedness of consciousness. It invades the deserter inimically, crippling and beclouding her; and so the woman becomes "one who is sleeping." Theseus, the embodiment of consciousness, leaves her. Her forlorn condition shows that she is threatened by *spiritual death,* as Jung formulated it in the previous quotation. This feeling of death, this situation of isolation is terrible, but it is also healing: it is the *pressure* that can lead to transformation. For the person who realizes the pressure with terror, Naxos becomes the divine or heavenly island – Dis, as it is also named. It is then holy, as helpfully nurturing as a Hermetic vessel. But this healing can take effect only when a person takes part in the event and of his free will enlists in it, as is symbolized by Ariadne when she hangs herself on the island. She knows inwardly not only her hanging and her fear: she has inner knowledge also of her human guilt. She is forsaken because she herself has forsaken her origin.

The image of hanging oneself is an image of breathtaking remorse and, at the same time, of breathtaking longing for the darkness of the psyche which was rejected. And the dumb cry of deadly longing is answered. Dionysus approaches: the psyche is animated in the convulsive dawn of new light that indeed no longer arises from the world but from the sea of the unconscious. This union is the central symbol of the Self in which light and darkness, the divine-demonic and the human are reconciled. The transformation of Ariadne consists of this: she is clarified and becomes clearly visible; this process is a symbol of becoming conscious. Dionysus, at the same time, changes from the bull-god into the god of wine. Formerly, he had affected human beings only through the fire of animal emotions; now he could be experienced in the glow of religious feeling, and the human heart can beat in unison with the All-Heart. This signifies a rebirth for the god also, when a human being becomes mother to him, for only in the religious experience of a human being does the divine-demonic – that is, the unconscious aspect of the psyche – become real.

The symbolism of the ascension surely points to Dionysian enthusiasm as an experience of being carried away. Another tradition, that of the crown of Ariadne, is more important for our purposes, that is psychologically. The golden crown is a *rotundum* and a costly jewel which Ariadne received from Dionysus at the very beginning. It is a symbol of the Self that has always been latent in human beings as a possibility for individuation. As Jung says in a note to the previously quoted excerpt from *Psychology and Alchemy:* "This does not mean that the self is created, so to speak, only during the course of life; it is rather a question of its becoming conscious. *The self exists from the very beginning,* but is latent, that is, *unconscious.*"[12] The symbol of the crown of Ariadne means exactly this. It was always there, but when Dionysus throws it into Heaven as a memorial to Ariadne (as its own memorial, that is), then it is visible as a guiding star. The lower, unconscious origin appears above as the conscious *goal.* This happening – the goal's becoming visible – is something that Ariadne, an earthly creature, cannot accomplish alone. It *happens* to her – *deo adiuvante* (God helping).

In this connection it is perhaps interesting to compare the paths of the women figures who belong to the family of Pasiphaë. Besides Pasiphaë herself and her two daughters, we can also include Medea, who was her niece (daughter of her brother Aietes).

As we have already seen, Pasiphaë embodies the primeval condition of unconsciousness that resembles paradise, insofar as *the problem of guilt plays no part.* At this level guilt cannot yet arise. All beings, all life, and all destruction are embedded in the eternally circling rhythm of *totality,* in which the divine, the human, and the animal – the good and the bad – are contained alike. The instincts rule, without consciousness interfering, and they take care that, as animals (bull and cow) meet for mating, so the natural course can proceed unbroken in the generations that follow. As there is no guilt in this paradisaic, primeval condition, so too there is only imperceptible development of nature over thousands of years. The individual being does not change. It is only part of the totality which is one and all.[13] The primeval condition of Pasiphaë is the archaic basis of feminine being in all times. The chthonic paradise of Crete opens to every woman who innocently gives birth to life and the destruction of life, at the same time as she gives birth to her children. There are many women even today who in their depths remain imprisoned in the Cretan paradise of primeval motherly unconsciousness, who know no guilt, and whose development advances only through their children.

The first step beyond this primeval condition is represented in Pasiphaë's daughter Phaidra. She abandons Crete and hurries without interruption in *one* direction, that is, toward Athens, in order to be queen there at the side of Theseus. Led by Theseus, she dissolves entirely into the consciousness given by her time and her world. She is then *only* conscious, but she has not become herself; she has become conscious only as the world is conscious. Psychologically expressed, this means that she has become identified with a *role* appropriate to the world. Complete accord with the world gives her a royal security which is only an apparent, surface one. Phaidra, in her one-sided development, has forgotten her origin: she no longer thinks about the fact that she is a daughter of Pasiphaë. This suppression of primitive instinctual nature and of the instincts then must avenge itself as soon as its primitive femininity is touched upon and stirred up. This, the myth represents by Phaidra's guilty love for her stepson Hippolytus. She desires the pure youth, who is entrusted to her motherliness. He, however, in pious reserve withdraws from her. This proves that neither Theseus nor Hippolytus turns out to mean anything to Phaidra. She thinks only of herself. As soon as she is crossed, her love turns to hate; she tells Theseus that Hippolytus has waylaid her. Hippolytus is executed by the outraged father, and Phaidra executes herself by hanging.

This is a monumental horror story, of which famous variations exist in many lands. It shows how terribly people in all times and places have been marked by the consequences of suppression. The primitive being is indeed always at the base of our humanity, even if it is suppressed. But through suppression, the basic becomes savage, barbaric, destructive. If it is then ripped up, through an outbreak of passion, the woman is no longer able to play the royal, conscious role that she has played. She is devoured by the Moloch of unconsciousness and sinks into a regression, just as Phaidra, through her blind, instinctual greed, is actually pulled back into the labyrinth of the Minotaur, her half-brother.

Phaidra's pathway shows the reeling of the egotistical woman from one extreme to the other. Because she sees only herself and follows only her own wishes, she cannot have inner knowledge of her guilt. Her hanging is not, as with Ariadne, an image of repentance. It is the ultimate phenomenon of egoism that can only assert itself through self-destruction.

In Pasiphaë also, feminine egoism is present, but it is guiltless, like everything of a primeval nature. In Phaidra, however, in whom a certain consciousness already exists, egoism becomes conscious along with the mania to elevate and gratify one's own ego. Phaidra, therefore, represents the problem of feminine egoism which is also present as a counter-current in the altruistic woman who rejoices in sacrifice, in whom it can break through suddenly if she does not become conscious of it. In the "labyrinth of her bosom," every woman houses a Minotaur.

The history of Medea presents an entirely different problem, the problem of *projection*. Just as Phaidra is her mother's daughter and thereby appears exposed to the problem of instinctual drive, so Medea is her father's daughter. Therefore, the paradise from which she springs has a masculine-intellectual character, in contrast with a Cretan one. The Colchis of Aietes on the Black Sea is also a place of archaic darkness. But here the garden of Aietes corresponds to the labyrinth of the Minotaur, the garden in which a dragon guards the primeval light of the golden fleece. The golden fleece is a sun-symbol; it stands for the primeval, magical knowledge of ancient people, which expresses their experience of totality. Since Medea, as her father's daughter, is connected with it, she is a magician. She knows a great deal, though without knowing herself.

When the representative of consciousness in the figure of the hero Jason rises to the surface in this magic realm, a dissolution begins. The negative, destructive side of the magic spirit is differentiated from the positive; Jason, as consciousness, helps Medea see through the destructive dragon – the symbol of black magic (the symbol for consciousness is the penetrating sword of the hero). Then, fleeing from Colchis, Medea *gives* Jason the golden fleece. That means she projects the light of the archaic spirit on him. Thereby, at the same time, she overvalues consciousness, as embodied in Jason; she takes it for the entire, autonomous spirit. This entails a loss for her. As the myth relates, Medea, in flight with Jason, must sacrifice her brother, Absyrtus, and cast him into the Black Sea of the unconscious. Absyrtus represents Medea's own capacity for insight, and this she loses because of her projection.

So Medea's way is different from Phaidra's. Certainly her development in consciousness is not as one-sided and over-emphasized as Phaidra's. She does not succeed in reaching Greece itself, but only Thessaly, a border province where, along with the light of consciousness, the darkness of the primeval condition is still alive. Medea therefore does not become entirely untrue to her origin.

But in Thessaly Jason leaves her; she is then a forsaken woman, like Ariadne on Naxos. But what happens? The mechanism of the projection, which is the determining factor in Medea, retains the upper hand. As she had formerly projected total light upon Jason, she now projects total darkness upon him: he is to blame for everything; he is evil. *The continuing projection prevents her from know-*

ing her own guilt and her own evil, and precisely through this she falls prey to the evil. Just as Phaidra regressed and fell prey to the Minotaur, so Medea is devoured by that which she imagined she had conquered, that is, by the dragon in the garden of her father Aietes. Through vain selfishness, Phaidra succumbs to the destructive side of nature; through limitless projection Medea succumbs to the destructive side of the autonomous spirit. She becomes a bride of the dragon, that is, a black magician. The deserted Medea is the most famous of the famous Thessalian witches. Her way ends in spiritual ruin. (Compare the exceptionally lively account of the myth of Medea in Ovid's *Metamorphoses.*)

Ariadne's way is very similar to that of Medea. Rising consciousness, embodied in Theseus, leads her too to a coming to terms, through which the labyrinth of instinctual drive is penetrated. One version of the Ariadne myth relates that she was able to accomplish this task of penetration with the help of a red thread; another says that the light-giving crown, which Dionysus had given her at the very beginning, provided light for her. Both symbols mean basically the same thing – that is, that Ariadne lets herself be guided purely by her feminine instincts, by the paths that are laid out already in childhood like a red thread or a guiding light. The instincts are the archetypal possibilities of right conduct through which, in unconscious people, the Self (in our myth, Dionysus) manifests itself. In Ariadne's first steps toward development, neither magic nor projection plays a part. She "remains with herself," as she does also when she goes the way of consciousness. What happens to her is an all-too-human error: misguided by consciousness, she overvalues *herself.* She does not see that the instincts, as a manifestation of the Self, signify a gift of God. She thinks, like all people whom consciousness impresses, that *I* did well, there *I* kept my nose clean. With this attitude, she does not appreciate the divinity of instinctual nature; she becomes untrue to her father-bridegroom, Dionysus as bull-god. *He* is the light of the earth; she does not possess it herself.

Like Medea, Ariadne does not go very far in her development toward consciousness. When only halfway there, she becomes a forsaken woman. But her death and her becoming clarified as Aridela on Naxos indicate that inwardly she knows and acknowledges the narrowness of consciousness. The defining factor is that she does not fall into projection like Medea but *that she comes to know her guilt,* is pierced by it, and accepts it. She does not despair about the world or about people. She doubts herself and despairs about herself. She has inner knowledge of her human nothingness. But as soon as she becomes nothing, the Self can again mean everything for her. The Naxos of Ariadne is a holy island because it represents the *deepest place* where the insight of guilt brings the annihilation of all identification with the "I" and where all energies are fixed upon the super-personal. Where the "I" is dead the Self becomes alive. In a powerful enantiodromia, the divine-demonic aspect of the psyche becomes manifest as Dionysus. The marriage of Dionysus and Ariadne on Naxos is so great a symbol of the *conjunctio* because *the moment of transformation in the individuation process* is therein held fast. In this image, everything is contained in one dynamic, moving reversal. Life becomes death and death becomes life, the human becomes godlike and the divine shows itself in human form, the animal takes unto itself spirit, and the hidden origin rises shining as the visible goal.

In these associations with myths we have already, it seems to me, the first evidence in favor of our working hypothesis. At any rate, it is certain that one cannot even try to understand the frescoes of the Villa of Mysteries if one does not have in mind the myth of Dionysus and Ariadne and its meaning. Each thing first becomes meaningful when it is regarded from the perspective of this central symbolism. For every woman who set foot in the Initiation Chamber of the Villa, Ariadne was a prototype; and for every one, this chamber could become a Naxos if she went without reservation through the narrow portal into the vessel of transformation. But – no woman thereby became an Ariadne herself for, as shown earlier, the prototype is thought of as *invisible.* The participant in the mystery could only follow it, and how she relived this mystery is represented, it seems to me, in the remaining scenes of the fresco series, as separate steps of a religious drama.

The Sacred Drama in the Villa of Mysteries

The First Scene

Jung writes of the alchemists whose *opus* certainly represents individuation symbolism:

> The alchemists themselves warned us: "*Rumpite libros, ne corda vestra rumpantur*" (Rend the books, lest your hearts be rent asunder), and this despite their insistence on study. *Experience,* not books, is what leads to understanding.[14]

Exactly the same can be asserted in principle about all classical mystery cults. Every such cult was a *mystery* because the drama of the cult was a deep secret that could not be exploited; as the Greeks also said, the mystery is an *arrhēton,* that is, something ineffable. The experience could not be expressed in words. Even now, not the book, but the *tradition* through holy writings is an essential part of every mystery cult.

With this initial statement, we come to the first scene of the fresco series. It must be said in advance that I shall not speak about the *colors* of the frescoes. It does not seem probable to me that one could discover what those who practiced the cult really thought about every single color. The background of the pictures is the familiar Pompeiian red.

The first two scenes will be discussed as briefly as possible. They have the character of an exposition and affect one as somewhat dry. Only with the third scene does the true mystery drama begin to flow, and then, step by step, it increases more and more in depth, significance, and intensity.

The initiate is depicted in this first scene as just having set foot in the chamber. She stands motionless and listens to a naked boy who, with an anxious expression on his face, reads from a scroll. As he does so, he is guided and protected by the priestess who sits behind him.

Let us turn first to the figure of the initiate. She wears the clothing of a Roman matron; a veil covers her head and back. She has supported her right hand lazily on her hip, and with the left she lifts the drapery over her bosom. This veil made earlier interpreters think of a wedding veil. Of this interpretation, we can only ask, who is the bridegroom? The veil screens the initiate from the *world,* which lies behind her. Undoubtedly, this is important to note. At the time of antiquity, life was much more collective than we can imagine. People lived entirely in the cheery hubbub of their groups. Those of the upper classes lived in large organizations of family and slaves (the latter were indeed also partly educated people). The aristocratic Roman woman was not only a society woman, she was also the responsible superintendent of the often large businesses where the household goods were produced. Everything, so to speak, was done in common; for example, people always bathed in common. I do not believe that the Romans would have summoned the energy solely for themselves alone to air themselves and scrub daily as zealously as was done in the common baths, where each gave wings to the pleasure of the other. In this style, community life was spent.

To turn aside from the group, therefore, and to conceal oneself from it – even if only for a while – surely signified a decisive change. It produced, indeed, a state of having been forsaken, in which the voice of the world was silent and the initiate's own voice, too, no longer penetrated. As a matter of fact, we do not know if this step of the initiation was preceded by a time of isolation, as was the case in many old initiations. But such an isolation is typical of the beginning of the way of individuation. Modern people experience it inwardly; this is no less terrible, and it is mirrored very often in dreams such as the ones Jung uses in the study of individual dream symbolism in *Psychology and Alchemy.*

What the gesture of the initiate means is not known. But one may perhaps note something about its symbolism. The right hand, resting on the hip, indicates *non-action;* lifting the drapery over the breast, on the other hand, indicates that the heart is opened to new impressions. The whole deportment of the initiate represents a *reposed collectedness,* and this attitude, too, is typical for the beginning of the way of individuation. The initiate is concentrating on the teaching which she receives from the lips of a child. That it is a child who instructs the initiate seems especially moving when we think that the motherhood of the woman of antiquity remained unconsciously in thrall to nature. Perhaps for the first time, the woman here sees the child not solely as the natural object of her nurturing instinct, but more importantly as the suffering bearer of divine meaning. Many ideas are similar: one could think also of the visit of the twelve-year-old Jesus to the temple, which forms a certain parallel to this scene.

Everywhere in the world, a *teaching* belonged to every initiation, which consisted of the ritual telling of sacred myths. The Greek word *mythologein* means just such a telling through which the myth as word (Logos) can become alive in the heart of the listener. In this respect the myth is the *theoria,* that is, the perception which brings about inner knowledge and which forms the hypothesis of religious practice. The *theoria* of the Orphic cult was the myth of the horrible death of Zagreus and of his rebirth, and it is obviously this myth which the boy in our scene has to read. The anxious expression on his face doubtless results from the fact that he feels sympathy during the religious reading and, at the same time, fear. He is therefore also the bearer of the pious feeling that likewise belongs at the beginning of the initiation and which he mediates to the initiate.

But the boy means still more than this. He is naked, which for the people of antiquity was a sign of the divine. And he wears the *cothurni.* (The *cothurni* [high laced boots] belong to the Greek theater that arose from the cult of Dionysus. It also appears, however, as an attribute of Dionysus. For example, there is a statue of a Dionysian sacrificial calf with *cothurni,* which show that in the animal the god himself is being sacrificed.) Because he wears the *cothurni,* he stands for Dionysus as a child, who himself brings the teaching through the child's mouth. The boy is the central symbol in the first scene. He is, if one may say so, the Angel of the Orphic Annunciation – pure, unadulterated innocence in which the divine word is not troubled by the influence of human thought.

Therefore the priestess does not speak in this first scene. She looks on; she is the representative of *consciousness,* which must also be there so that living the initiation proceedings does not only happen but becomes conscious as well. Her attentive glance is directed toward the gesture of the initiate as she lifts the drapery over her breast. It is as if the priestess is inquiring, has this heart been opened to the divine heartbeat?

The Second Scene

The transition to the second scene is made by the figure of the initiate, adorned with the crown of myrtle, who now goes further on her way. She seems still to be harkening back to the teaching which she has just heard. She has let her cloak fall; under it one sees a light, sleeveless tunic. She carries a sliced, sacrificial cake in a metal vessel in her left hand, for which reason Maiuri describes her as the "sacrificer." With her right hand she holds a small branch of laurel near the vessel.

Leopold Feiler, who in spite of his enthusiasm never lost the sharp eye of a doctor, noticed at once the remarkable contours of her figure.[15] He says the woman looks pregnant, the way the folds of her coat and tunic are lifted over her body. After closer scrutiny, he then states that no, under the tunic the body is quite slim; it is, therefore, only an apparent pregnancy. This extremely noteworthy fact makes us think back to the first scene where the initiate, ready to receive, has lifted the garment over her heart. Now we see: *something* really has penetrated her and sunk into the very depths of her bowels – something invisible, insubstantial, by which she has now become pregnant.

In this connection, Feiler also considered old usages which belonged to the cult of Sabazios. Sabazios is the Phrygian form of Dionysus, and it is from there that the musical instruments, flutes and cymbals, entered the cult of Dionysus. In the cult of Sabazios, in the course of the initiation, a snake was pulled through the garment of the participant in the mystery – a snake which represented the god. It was in connection with this rite that the god was called *ho dis kolpou theos*—the god who goes through the bosom. "To take into the bosom" was, besides, a conventional Greek expression for conception.

We can adopt this symbolism here, for the representations of the initiate in the first two scenes show that such ideas must have had at least a part in our mystery cult; we shall see that the snake symbol emerges again later. Whether something comparable to the Phrygian rite was performed at the Villa of Mysteries, we naturally do not know. It could also be that the archaic-concrete Phrygian form of the rite in the Villa found a symbolically refined form. This, however, does not matter. The essential thing is the connection which the frescoes offer: that Dionysus, who at first appeared as the holy word, is suddenly presented as a snake.

The *snake symbol* plays a very important part in the cult of Dionysus. The basis of the snake ritual in the cult of Sabazios is the myth that Zeus, as he begot Zagreus, approached Persephone in the form of a snake. The snake ritual perpetuates the memory of this myth and, at the same time, portrays the participant in the role of Kore-Persephone. As this goddess, she conceives and then carries the future divine child—invisible, insubstantial—in herself. In the Orphic cult, it is just that part of the myth referring to the conception of Zagreus which is surrounded with mystery. There is an Orphic saying that reads: "The bull as father begat the snake, and the snake is the father of the bull."

This is the primeval conception that is found in the myths of many peoples, according to which the God of Creation is his own begetter—or the first cause of his own genesis. In this sense, the Orphic cult defines Zagreus also as the pre-existent Dionysus: even before he was born, he was; and he receives his existence through himself alone.

We find similar concepts in alchemy where, indeed, they may lead to the most paradoxical statements. For example, there is an old recipe for making divine water, the original liquid form of the lapis, which says that one must, among other things, use divine water.[16] This means it can only be produced through itself. These are mythical substantiations which refer—as is the case with all myths

– to the contents of the collective unconscious: the *archetypes*. These are always there, and we could describe them as pre-existent, in that they are the constituents of all psychic life. Symbolically speaking, it is entirely fitting when an archetype and its corresponding image are defined as father and son. It is through the image alone that the archetype can be perceived; thus, seen from the point of view of human experience, it cannot be determined which was first. Both are the same: the begetter has begotten himself. The *image* that corresponds to an archetype can, however, take on the most diverse forms and still stand for the same primordial human method of control. When an archetypal image rises to the surface and the human being realizes its effect, he can probably never find out which was first, the image or its effect. It is, perhaps, on account of such perplexities that concepts as completely different as snake and bull are experienced and described as an impenetrable father-son unity.

The snake is an archetypal image so widespread that almost everyone knows something about it or has at least once had some inkling of its meaning. In almost all human beings, the sight of a snake arouses fear or a numinous feeling. We modern people, to be sure, usually see larger snakes only in zoological gardens. But to Romans they were both familiar and holy. As embodiments of the *lares* – that is, the forebears and guardians of the boundaries – they were, until a late period, kept as honored domestic animals.[17] It was considered a very bad omen when a house-snake died. This Roman usage preserves the religious ideas of many primitive peoples, who looked upon snakes as the reappearance of the dead and as bearers of healing or wisdom. The snake has always had *spiritual meaning*. Cold, damp, watery, strange, and dangerous, a snake embodies the sinister darkness of the unconscious psyche, but also the knowledge that is hidden there. Archaic people did not ascribe knowledge or wisdom to themselves; they came to know it as coming "from the other side," as the spirit of the dead, of ancestors, and thus as a secret of the night. As ruler of the dead and of the souls, the old Thracian Dionysus has the same meaning: he is the ancestral wisdom of all mankind and the knowledge of the universal soul. Therefore, snakes were carried in the processions of the Bacchantes also. For the Romans, then, these concepts could crystallize into the concept of the *lares*.

In the Orphic cult, the same connection between Dionysus and the snake is found. Indeed, it adds another dimension, so to speak, since Dionysus as Phanes signifies the new, that is, the *future* light. Phanes is represented as being entwined spirally by a snake. In this regard, I refer to Leisegang's beautiful essay "The Mystery of the Serpent," in which the multifarious references to this complicated and philosophically extended symbolism are handled in detail. In the image of Phanes, the light of the past appears changed into future light, the origin appears as goal – both united through the spiral way of the snake. Everything in this symbolism is Dionysian, and everything is light, mystic sun. As a verse attributed to Orpheus expresses it:

> Hear, thou who turnest forever the radiant
> sphere of distant motion
> that runs round the celestial vortices,
> glittering *Zeus Dionysus,* father of the sea,
> father of the earth, sun,
> all-engendering, all-moving, flaming with gold.[18]

This all-powerful sun symbol points to the Self and, with the swinging way of the circle or the spiral, points at the same time toward the process of becoming a Self. Christ, who according to the Gospel of John is origin, light, and life, also has the snake as symbol. But whereas the light of Christ comes from above, Dionysus's light always comes from below. We shall see later what a great difference it makes whether the Self is experienced as a light from Heaven, or as a light from the earth, or from the underworld.

Something of the rich symbolic content which I have tried to point out here, as represented in our frescoes, penetrated the initiate of the Orphic mystery cult of the Pompeiian villa. She becomes pregnant with it, enlightenment stirs in her, but at first invisibly, in her bowels. This is like bodily occurrences through which the snake symbol manifests itself. Even today, for example, we see the snake in dreams – that is, in emotional states – when the restraining influence of brain activity (principally of the cerebrum) on the deeper nerve centers falls into abeyance. Thereby functioning becomes purely reflexive, and one carries on more or less blindly. In this connection it is interesting to recall the notion of ancient times and of the Middle Ages, that real snakes are born from the human spinal cord, for reflex action is characteristic of the spinal cord. At the same time, the lower, older nervous system gains the upper hand. The consequence of this situation is phenomena of excitement, which are bound up on the one hand with bodily symptoms (palpitating heart, stomach and intestinal disturbances, and sexual stimulation), and, on the other hand, with a flood of ideas. There are Negro tribes who say: "I have anxiety in the bowels" and thereby precisely localize bodily symptoms which accompany emotions. It is the same for us. As soon as our emotions get the upper hand, we feel it in our bowels. We can no longer think sensibly. "The old snake" governs us again; we act blindly and are carried away.

This is enough, surely, to show what it means when Dionysus "goes through the bosom" of a human being as a snake. It signifies an agitation of emotions which, no matter how uncomfortable it may be, can still be healing, since meaning can be hidden behind the flooding concepts that are tied up with it. Pregnancy through the snake, which our fresco apparently represents, is in quite common speech what we still call a *Dionysian mood,* in which fear and hope are mixed in a way which shakes us up. Such a state of mind can be of the greatest value, because the condition of being all tied up in knots, that otherwise might hinder one, can suddenly fall away.

It was not very different for the Romans than it is for us. Although they were much more unrestrained than we are in many ways and more primitive – with their mad, noisy festivals, their terrible orgies of eating, and their fear of spirits and ghosts – their position as world rulers demanded an extremely strict adaptation. The larger the human world becomes, the more it invades a person with demands and pressures; so much the more must each individual protect himself through the development of that firm outer form which we today designate by the psychological term of *persona*. We need only observe the numerous portrait busts and statues of

Romans which remain to realize how impressive, how close to perfect their personas were. They could not compensate this outer rigidity through attacks of blind abandonment to nature; they could only conquer it from *within* through the experience of true *ecstasy,* that is, through a Dionysian state of mind.

But as we already saw in the first scene of our fresco series, preparation is needed for such ecstasy; one must go in search of it, and one must do it in the right place and at the right time. For the boiling up of emotions is also something very dangerous; indeed, one can never know how far it will sweep one away and whether one may not be driven to panic or to orgiastic wantonness. The great danger of the cult of Dionysus was that it could turn to orgiastic excesses and destructive ravings. This same danger exists today too, wherever masses of people are emotionally seized and carried away. It can only too easily result in a monumental hangover or even a catastrophe.

Ecstasy is always a sign that an archetype has been constellated or, to remain with our symbolism, that the god has appeared as a snake. If it is to be meaningfully experienced, a set form is needed which offers protection. Here, it is the religious framework of the Initiation Chamber, in which the excess of boiling emotion can be caught and transformed through a *sacrifice.* Sacrifice is indeed the most important element in all religious cultures. It indicates that the human being in the midst of his ecstasy recognizes and honors the power that seizes him, even when it remains invisible to his eyes. Then the storm quiets down, and there remains the bridal hope and tender awe with which the human being, swollen with expectation, can go to meet the unknown in a religious spirit. Thus we see the woman offering sacrifice in our fresco series. Adorned with the crown of myrtle, carrying the sacrificial vessel in her hands – the vessel which as sacrificial gift contains a cake cut into pieces – she goes serenely to the altar table to bring her gift.

When the woman who is making the sacrifice arrives at the altar table, a ritual is already under way. So we must first speak about that proceeding. Then we shall speak again about the sacrificial gift. First, I will simply describe the scene at the altar.

The dignity of the priestess who presides over the proceedings at the altar is emphasized by her elevated seat, covered with beautiful cloth, which is like a primitive throne. She is also crowned with a crown of myrtle. At her left is a maidservant with a covered basket that seems to be heavy, for while she holds it toward the priestess, she has to support it on her knee. At the right of the table is a younger priestess, aslo crowned with myrtle, who carries a scroll inside her cloak. She has brought a small basket which now stands before her on the table. What we can see of the ritual proceeding is as follows:

The dominant woman, whom perhaps we can designate as high priestess, holds a twig of laurel over the small basket at the right, and the younger priestess pours holy water over it from a little jug. At the same time, with her other hand, the high priestess slightly lifts the cover of the large, heavy basket at her left. Maiuri suggests that this manner of representation could show that the high priestess intends to lay the sprig of laurel in the large basket, after it has been purified with the holy water. As will perhaps be remembered, the woman making the sacrifice brings a similar twig of laurel together with the cake, so that it looks as though the same procedure will follow. This much is certain: the proceedings at the altar table have to do with the large basket at the left; consecrated twigs are brought and laid in it.

We shall therefore speak at once about the symbol of this basket. This is also the easiest way to understanding, for we are dealing here with a well-known symbol of the Roman cult of Bacchus. Such a Dionysian basket is found, for example, on coins and on objects of the Orphic cult, and also on a mural of the Villa of Mysteries outside the Initiation Hall. In these representations, the basket is open a little and a snake peers out. On the basis of these parallels, we can safely designate the basket as a Dionysian *kista mystika* (mystical basket) which contains the god as snake.

Since we have already spoken about the snake symbol, the image of the *kista mystika* is the only new element. I will cite very briefly a relevant episode from the myths. According to one version of the myth, the dismembered Dionysus was brought back to life by a mother goddess (different names are cited). Then the Great Mother Cybele, who instructed him in his mystery cult, also gave him the implements for it. At the same time, she purified him for his cult.

The *kista mystika* with the snake in it is the *central symbol* in our second scene; it gives significance to the whole proceeding at the altar table. Here the high priestess is represented as enthroned because she takes the place of the Great Mother; she consecrates into the cult the woman taking part in the mystery, just as the goddess once consecrated Dionysus. The symbol of the laurel twigs is to be understood primarily in this connection. They are the young, budlike, psychic growth that appears everywhere in the symbol of plants. The twigs represent the souls of the participants in the mystery – or the Dionysian spark in them – which are here purified by the libation and given up to the god.

This is easily said, but like everything symbolic, it is not easily understood and raises various questions. What does it mean in reality when the soul is given over to the god in *this* form, that is, as snake in the *kista mystika?* What sort of gift did Cybele offer to Dionysus with the *kista mystika?* And where does the symbol of the fragmented sacrificial cake belong in this instance? These are all questions that one can only meditate upon and – perhaps – answer, step by step.

The *kista mystika,* like all symbols of this sort – for example, the basket of Moses, the chest in which Osiris floated over the sea, or even any "burial tree" in which a human being awaits his resurrection – is a symbol of the *mother* as protector and preserver. With the *kista mystika,* the Great Mother Cybele gives herself to Dionysus, like a bride whom he as bridegroom has penetrated. He is not seen, but everything is hopeful, everything is bride-like, for indeed, he is not dead: he lives in the bride-like mother.

When the god in our fresco series appears as a central symbol in the form of a snake, he is the light hidden in the Great Mother *Nature* (or Cybele). In nature a human being has his first inkling of the divine; creative force first becomes reality through nature's sacred order, where the permanence in fluctuation of the interacting shape of things seems to reveal knowledge and carry meaning. It is, therefore, as though the ***kista mystika,*** in the second fresco scene, indicates the next step to the initiate, as though it would say: seek in nature and thou shalt find the god.

But where then does the symbol of the sacrificial cake belong? To pursue this question we must ascertain something further. We are indeed concerned with a sacrament, and even the simplest sacramental ceremony comprises a great deal. As I said earlier, the basis of the Orphic mystery cult was the myth of Zagreus, who was dismembered and eaten by the Titans. Human beings were said to originate from the ashes of the punished Titans and, thereby, inherit their nature and their guilt. The fragmented cake is indeed something edible that has been "dismembered" so that it could be ritually eaten. This fact reminds us that in the old Greek Orphic cults there already were such rites. The followers of the old Orphic religion were not allowed to eat meat because Zagreus also had animal forms. But once a year they came together to a sacramental meal; they tore raw meat to pieces with their hands and ate it. In this way they imitated the legendary Maenads, who in homage stormed through the forests after Dionysus in holy frenzy, tearing wild creatures to pieces with their hands and eating them. There are other old legends along the same lines which relate that mothers tore their own children to pieces in Dionysian frenzy.

It seems certain that the Dionysian animal sacrifice, in its turn, succeeded the human sacrifice of archaic times. The cult of Dionysus has a very ancient background. Rumors of human sacrifice, therefore, were still connected with this cult in Roman times. It was on account of such a rumor, for example, that the cult was forbidden in Rome in the second century B.C. It is noteworthy that it is in connection with the legends mentioned above that Dionysus was called *Omēstēs* (the devourer), as though it were he who tore the Maenads to pieces, whereas it was they who tore him to pieces in his animal form. In this instance, the legendary Maenads are supposed to have been clothed in the bloody hides of dismembered animals; they therefore actually appeared as these animals. Everything is interwoven here to the point of indistinguishability, and in the final analysis the sacrificer and the sacrifice are one.

In the legends of the Maenads, in the sacramental feasts of the old Greek Orphic rites, human beings appeared simultaneously in the role of Titans, who dismembered Zagreus. Through religious ceremonies – be it in the archaic, orgiastic form or in the form modified by developed religion, the form of the sacrament – the Titan nature and the original sin of human beings become manifest; that is, they reenact the experience of the mythical prototype. But in the sacramental meal, the human being no longer acts blindly. The significance of every sacrament is that the person thereby has a religious experience, as the god fills him with the sacrificial food and becomes savior to him; or, as the Orphics specifically taught, Dionysus frees the human soul from conflict with the savagery of his nature.

It is similar in our second fresco scene, when the woman making the sacrifice brings the green twig for purification along with the sliced cake, so that later it can be given to the god. Surely it was she herself who had cut the cake ritually, so she herself was thereby placed symbolically in the role of the Titan. One need not wonder that in the Pompeiian private cult, a kind of bread replaced raw meat; indeed, we know of other cults too where, in the course of time, the sacrifice became less and less gross and concrete, where a cultivated product of the earth replaced the mere animal. The basic meaning remains the same. Besides, for the Romans, the cake was the accepted substitute for the meat, for cakes were used also in ancestor worship; this is especially meaningful for our discussion when we think that the Roman *lares* also took snake form.

While the god is represented as still invisible in the woman making the sacrifice, ruling in her bowels, yet in the sacramental meal – in the eating of the sliced, sacrificial cake, which clearly follows at the altar table after the blessing of the twig – the god is already received on a higher plane, namely, in the *stomach* of the human being. In the body's household, the stomach is the kitchen where food is made ready for digestion. Eating and digestion are primeval symbols, a fact which we still know and use in colloquial speech. They describe a kind of experience which no longer consists only of emotional ecstasy, but of a slow *process* whereby contents are truly "swallowed" and incorporated into one's own being. The "swallowing" in this case means a willing assimilation, and the "digestion," a gradual integration of what the swallowed contents mean, in and for one's self.

I had great difficulty describing the symbolism of the ritual ceremony at the altar table both comprehensibly and briefly, for I had, purely and simply, to delineate details of action which are more or less subtle, ones which are sometimes simultaneous and, at any rate, all run into each other. This was also a kind of "dismemberment," and, therefore, we too must try to understand what the symbolic proceedings at the altar table may mean from a psychological standpoint.

From such a perspective then, we start with the myth of the Titans and with their inherited guilt. The Titans were the children of Gaia, that is, of the earth, and they were also the first rulers over the earth. Not until the next generation of gods do the Olympians arise. They conquer the Titans in a long, terrible fight, making them prisoners under the mountains which they heap over them. But there the Titans remain alive, making themselves felt in the heavy rumbling of earthquakes and the eruption of volcanoes. As symbols, the Titans stand for primitive instinctuality and burning lust which are masters of all earthbound creatures. The Olympians, however, who came into being later, embody various aspects of conscious spirit, which must conquer wild drives and even crush them while creating order and continuity. But the drives are not rooted out by this conscious spirit. Just as the Titans make the earth quake and cause fiery eruptions from their prisons, so too, again and again, under the reign of the spirit that has become conscious, instinctuality which has been forcibly tamed can break out, explosive and fiery. With the Olympian victory of the spirit, therefore, the problem of instinctuality and desirousness is not solved; it is only put off.

Therefore, according to Orphic tradition, Zeus created Dionysus; he planned to make him ruler over the earth. Here we see how the *intuition* of a unifying symbol originates in the conscious spirit, here embodied in Zeus. He created Dionysus, in whom light and darkness are united, to resolve the conflict of the opposites. But mere intuition – and that is really the pre-existent Dionysus-Zagreus – does not suffice; on the contrary, it only creates sharper conflict and disorder. The Titans break out, dismember Zagreus, and Zeus apparently must confess himself beaten. But now he answers the inimical stroke with a creative act which goes beyond mere intuition: he burns the Titans to ashes, and from these ashes human beings are created.

Up to now we have been concerned with a cosmic myth, which portrays the eternal conflict between spirit and matter. But now, with the creation of human beings, the same conflict is moved to a new level (namely, the human) and appears as an inner-human, microcosmic event. As in other myths also, human beings represent the solution for divine problems (for example, in many hero-myths). Here, too, the task of solving the primeval conflict between spirit and matter through human development is bequeathed to human beings as an inheritance. But what does it mean, from the point of view of human development, that the Titans devour the unifying symbol? It surely means that, for human beings too, a mere intuition of patterns of healing does not suffice: it creates only conflict and disorder. In consequence, it becomes all the clearer that, for human beings too, the highest value at first lies hidden *nolens volens* (willy-nilly, willing or not) in instinctuality and matter. It cannot be otherwise; it is the natural, youthful condition of all human beings that the drives and lusts are at first directive, imprisoning them in matter. Their first goal *is* the material world.

I once knew an Indian student who was also studying with a Yogi. The Yogi had first taught him Hatha (that is, bodily) Yoga and then said to him one day that this instruction was now finished and he, the student, might turn to a higher, spiritual level. He should think this over. The student did so and found there was still an unconquerable curiosity alive in him. This he confessed to his Yogi, and the latter judged that in this case the student simply was not yet done with the *eating of the world;* he must also eat his curiosity to the end and should therefore make a trip around the world. The student had no money, but nevertheless he started out. He earned his world trip by traveling from university city to university city, giving lectures and demonstrations on Hatha Yoga in medical departments. I met him while he was doing this – a modest, eager, and superb young Titan.

From this example, we can see how important for the development of the human being the "eating of the world" is considered by the old philosophy of the Indians. It is important for all human beings, but if this situation lasts and becomes one-sided, it leads to an *overvaluation* of instinctuality and matter. This we see, for example, precisely in the Roman civilization of Imperial times, where voluptuousness and worldly pleasure took unbridled command, so that, in late Roman life a terrible gulf opened between a truly Titanic greed and the Olympian order of consciousness, which manifested itself so surpassingly, for example, in Roman statecraft and Roman law. In the Middle Ages, the Titans seemed to be subdued and buried through real suppression. Therefore in this epoch, which was so extraordinarily cultivated intellectually, material man was a poor animal, neglected and dirty, a state which avenged itself again and again through vast eruptions. The conflict between the order of consciousness and instinctuality, which can express itself as either sensuality or inordinate desire for power, is a problem at every period of time, as it is today. The sciences have certainly produced a truly Olympian order in the modern world. But we need only look, for example, at cinema advertising to see that voluptuousness, sensationalism, and ostentatiousness rule the imagination; and the sort of explosions the Titanic desire for power calls forth in today's world, I certainly need not describe.

Overwhelming instinctuality is truly our inherited Titanic sin, and worldly life leads every single person into his fate at least once:

> Ihr führt ins Leben uns hinein,
> ihr lasst den Armen schuldig werden
> dann überlasst ihr ihn der Pein
> denn alle Schuld rächt sich auf Zerden.
>
> Thou carriest us into life
> thou allowest the poor soul to become guilty
> then givest him up to pain
> for all guilt revenges itself on earth.

The lightning of Zeus which shattered the greedy Titans is a symbol for that sudden insight into the senselessness of inordinate desire which can strike like a bolt of lightning, disgusting one with the one-sidedness of material life. The symbol shows also that such an insight signifies a creative deed, in that through it the human being first truly becomes human.

In our frescoes this insight is also represented symbolically in the sacramental proceedings of the second scene – namely, in the figure of the younger priestess, who pours out the holy water and at the same time carries a scroll. This figure corresponds to the priestess of the first scene, who is also an embodiment of consciousness, and to whom is given by tradition (that is, by the scroll) the knowledge that the soul troubled by guilt has need of purification. I will not say more about this here, for we shall see in the next scene how purification and transformation first fulfill themselves in our mystery.

In this regard, I should like to say just a word about the real meaning of the laurel twigs that are being purified and to which, as symbols of psychic growth, I have only alluded so far. From a psychological point of view, what can we understand about that which is freed when a human being sees through his Titan nature? It must be something that also belongs to his nature, something that was created with him or, in other words, that is given to him innately as his own highest value, corresponding to the Dionysian spark. Since laurel twigs are laid in the *kista mystika,* we can perhaps say that we are concerned with a psychic predisposition in human beings that is by nature turned toward the divine. We can call it the *religious instinct* that is laid down in every human being as an archetypal way of control, which he can follow as soon as he is freed from the inner dark caused by inordinate greed. When the instinct is confirmed in its purity, it is always the most dependable guide, for it is exactly adapted to eternal human necessities. The turn to the divine as an instinctive possibility is a very high value – at least according to the *consensus omnium* of all times. Whither it leads, to be sure, one perhaps cannot know by oneself; one needs a more highly placed, experienced person, who can direct one in relation to it. In our second fresco scene, the high priestess is this directing figure. She has, so to speak, an instinct-guidance within, and this leads the human being, prepared by Dionysus, not upward – as with Christians – but downward, to the light under the earth, symbolized by the *kista mystika*.

A great many modern people are no longer in the fortunate situation of being close to an archetypal religious tradition in which they can achieve insight and change. We have developed a strong, indeed a rigid, personal consciousness; therefore we must, perhaps, understand personally the problem of instinctuality and human guilt, from which no one is free. That is, we must recognize exactly where and how we have sunk into the drive for power or into lust; we must know for what guilt we are personally responsible, so the religious instinct can come into being and function freely and purely in us. For many modern people, therefore, the second scene of our fresco series corresponds to the search into the *personal* unconscious. But who would have thought the dull and extremely unpleasant occupation with the shadow side and the all-too-human in us could have meaning as a parallel to a mystery sacrament! And still it is so; it cannot be otherwise, for even we modern people cannot gain the vaguest insight into the personal unconscious if the good, ministering spirit does not bring us the *kista mystika* with the snake. To be sure, we do not see this in the ancient, concrete form; we too, however, need an experienced person of higher standing to direct us, because for us the mystical basket which conceals the snake-like divine content is the *dream*.

Differentiation between the personal and the collective unconscious has become necessary on account of the strongly marked development of consciousness in modern times. For the individual human being, this has led to an equally strongly marked development of conscious personality at the cost of all those elements of one's being that are felt to be unsuitable and are therefore neglected. So in the course of development, individuals must first draw up and integrate these contents of the personal unconscious in order to make their personalities whole. In this process, however, they come up against the contents of the *collective* unconscious also and experience that great "coming to terms" that we denote as the individuation process.

For the person of antiquity, the circumstances were not entirely the same. There, the unconscious was not so sharply separated from the conscious; its contents, in the form of legendary and mythical ideas, flowed continuously into its world view. People of antiquity experienced their human nature in such ideas – as, for example, in the Orphic idea of the Titan nature. What for us is the personal unconscious was for them the Titanic Chaos, in which, through a dismemberment (that is, a symbolic separation), they had to find the *prima materia,* if I may use this alchemical terminology. The *kista mystika* with the snake is parallel to the alchemical *prima materia*. As soon as the participant in the mystery came into relationship with it and participated in it, he found *prima materia* also in himself as the possibility of psychic growth beyond the chaotic condition of human beings as they are. Symbolically, this is represented by the green laurel twiglets. So through the mystery cults, a traditional form and method were given so that ancient people could see religiously through the chaos of the Titanic nature of humanity. It guided them almost unnoticeably and without strong personal conflicts up to the boundary of the collective unconscious. But then their problem became similar to ours; for them, too, there opened the unknown land of human dreams, with which they had to come to terms through an experience comparable to the modern individuation process. This we see represented in the remaining frescoes of our mystery cult, beginning with the third scene.

The Third Scene

After the second scene with its sacramental proceedings, we are removed, in the third, into a fairyland and therewith to a new level of experience. The human figures with their ritual and their religious objects suddenly disappear, and the secrets of nature become manifest: a Silenus crowned with myrtle plays ecstatically on a lyre, and fauns and kids near him rejoice in an idyllic togetherness.

We will speak first about the figure of the Silenus, which binds the second scene to the third. A cloak of soft lilac tone falls so that it covers only the lower half of his body. The symbol of half-nakedness points to the fact that Silenus is a half-divine being;

although rooted in the human, he in his ecstasy towers up into the divine and belongs to it. The soft corpulence that is a chief characteristic of the Silenus figure is especially prominent in our representation: he is almost repulsively spongy and fat.

Silenus is a constant companion of Dionysus. He was originally a fountain demon from whom wisdom flowed; therefore he was a watery spirit. At the same time, however, he was also a Dionysian wine demon who prophesied in drunkenness. He had the blood of the god in him. The fountain, which he embodies, is therefore a special *divine* spring. (As a parallel, the "divine water" of alchemy can be mentioned. Compare also page 72 below.) As the fountain of divine water, Silenus was also Dionysus's teacher. Symbolically, he is the embodiment of the holy water that purifies the laurel twiglets in the second scene. In the figure of Silenus this water has become alive; it flows out of him like a fresh fountain and murmurs in the soft tones of the lyre which he plays. This is the basic significance of Silenus and, at the same time, his divine side – the holy water that like wine works to enliven, to give wings.

If we wish to translate this symbolism into modern language, we can perhaps say it is related to the healing, purifying significance of the unconscious that achieves living efficacy. Water has always this meaning: it is the unconscious flowing. When the participants in the mystery come to the figure of Silenus on their way of initiation, they stand at the border, where the collective unconscious opens itself to them. Silenus is the mediator who first puts them in contact with the contents of the collective psyche.

He is therefore an extraordinarily important figure, and he has a comparably large number of very meaningful aspects. In ancient times, a special kind of Silenus figure was beloved – one that could be opened and which contained costly, small statues. They show that Silenus as mediator is also something like a *jewel box* which contains costly things. These flow from him through the wisdom which he makes known as the great teacher. To this aspect belongs the folk tradition that, when Silenus was drunk, he was fettered by the Bacchantes with chains of roses so that he would prophesy. He gives out his wisdom when surrounded by loving cajolery. This is the significance also of the incident in Plato's *Symposium* when, at the moment when the drunkenness of this winged evening reached its height, Alcibiades compared Socrates with the Silenus image in which, when one opens it, one glimpses statues of gods.[19]

The jewel box with its costly contents is a receptacle and therefore also a feminine symbol. It emphasizes the feminine, motherly aspect which already stands out in the soft corpulence of Silenus. This strikes one as extraordinarily archaic; and it truly seems to reach very far back, as one can gather from certain parallels. For example, in the Peloponnesian cult of Artemis Kordaka, the goddess was honored in an indecent sacred dance, the Kordax, by men disguised as fat women. Their paunches were their most conspicuous characteristic, as with Silenus. According to a communication from Professor Kerényi, the idea which the men embodied in the dance corresponds to those prehistoric female idols which were downright mountains of flesh, as can be seen in Greek vase paintings. These give an archaic, concrete representation of the overflowing bounteousness of All-mother Nature. This aspect of nature, and also dance, represents natural events which change from moment to moment, and they were represented by the old Kordax dancers of Diana (Artemis). These things were represented by the Silenus image also, but simultaneously with the idea that natural events enclose secret *significance,* like costly statues of gods. The statues of gods symbolize the meaning that can manifest itself in changing, flowing, dancing natural events. This idea was familiar to the ancients. The Latin concepts of the *omen* (the prognostication) and the *portentum* (the portent) express this idea, and on it all old methods of divination rested: for example, the sacrificial play or the flight of birds.

While the feminine aspect of Silenus (who, moreover, wears a crown of myrtle, like the women of the previous scene) symbolizes the bounteousness and the bride-like readiness of nature to receive, his masculine aspect is that of a priest, a diviner, who in trance can predict the meaning of natural events from moment to moment. This is also his more human side. In this respect, Silenus is perhaps to be compared with those medicine men of primitive tribes who wore women's clothing and pretended to be women just at the time when their function was a spiritual, guiding, teaching one. This disguise represented in entirely concrete form that, while these men mediated to the tribe the divine wisdom of the ancestors, they were only receptacles, only instruments for the superhuman powers that ruled them.[20]

At higher levels of culture there are similar views: for example, in China, where the meaning of constantly changing natural events has been grasped in the concept of *Tao*. Richard Wilhelm relates that he once asked a Chinese what that might be, that *Tao*, and thereupon the Chinese pointed to the view out the window and said: "All that, the trees, the meadows, the wind – everything that we see – is *Tao*." It is the events of nature, changing, dancing, that are always the manifestation of meaning, which changes in the same way. In this respect one might call the divine side of Silenus too an embodiment of *Tao;* but at the same time he is also, as the Chinese say, the noble one who understands the meaning of the event and can mediate and teach it.

Similar views existed also in Europe until modern times. Paracelsus, for example, expressed them through his idea that there are for human beings two sources of inner knowledge: one being God and the other being the *light of nature,* which makes it possible for plants and animals to make wisdom known to attentive human beings. The Silenus image which contains jewels is a symbol for the light of nature; at the same time, however, he is also the one that makes the light known. As such he is mother and father and mediator for those who participate in the Pompeiian cult. His fatherhood shows itself in further symbolism which likewise belongs to this many-layered image.

He is represented as playing the lyre. This instrument did not originally belong to Silenus; he took it over from the first teacher of the Orphics, Orpheus, who is supposed to have brought the secret cult of Dionysus to Greece. On the fresco of the Initiation Hall of the Villa, therefore, the figure of Silenus has blended with that of Orpheus. As representative of the first teacher, he embodies the *tradition* through which mystery wisdom is carried from generation to generation, from times as distant as Pompeii. It is an exceptionally important realization, found in many philosophies, that no single person "can suck wisdom from his fingers," so to speak. One must be guided by the experience of mankind, which is passed on from mouth to mouth, from master to pupil, and which contains the totality of the knowledge of life which the fragmentary, single

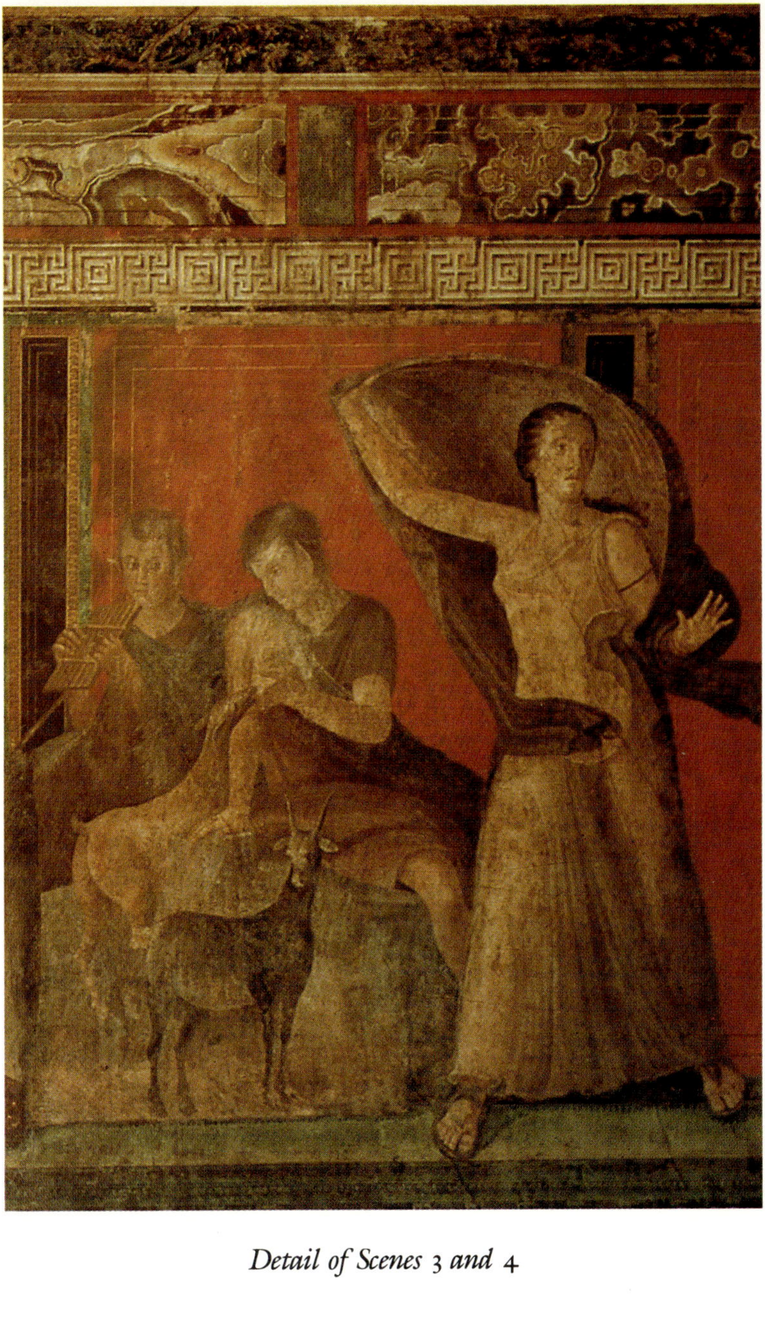

Detail of Scenes 3 and 4

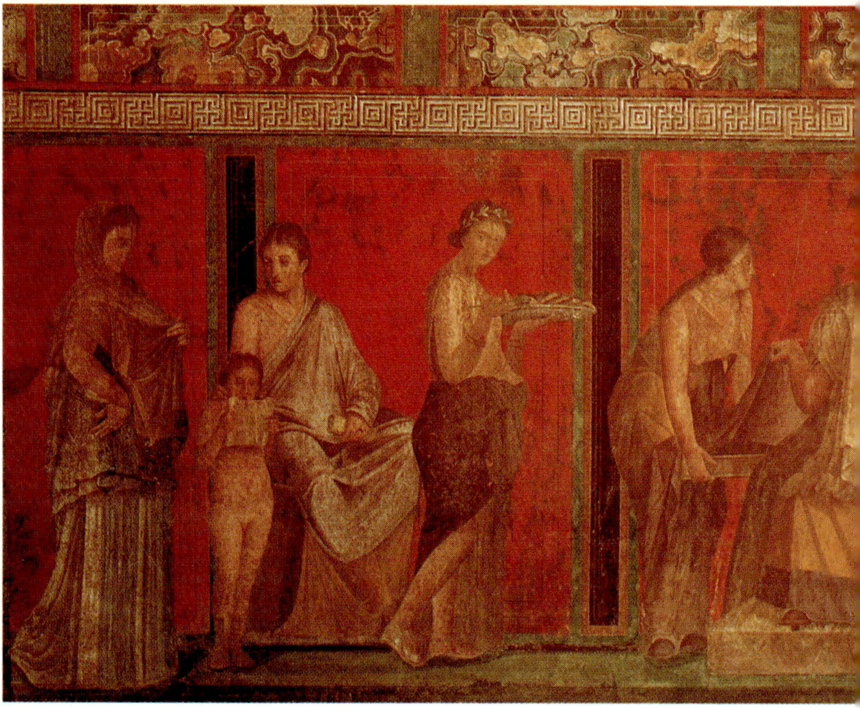

Scene 1 — Scene 2

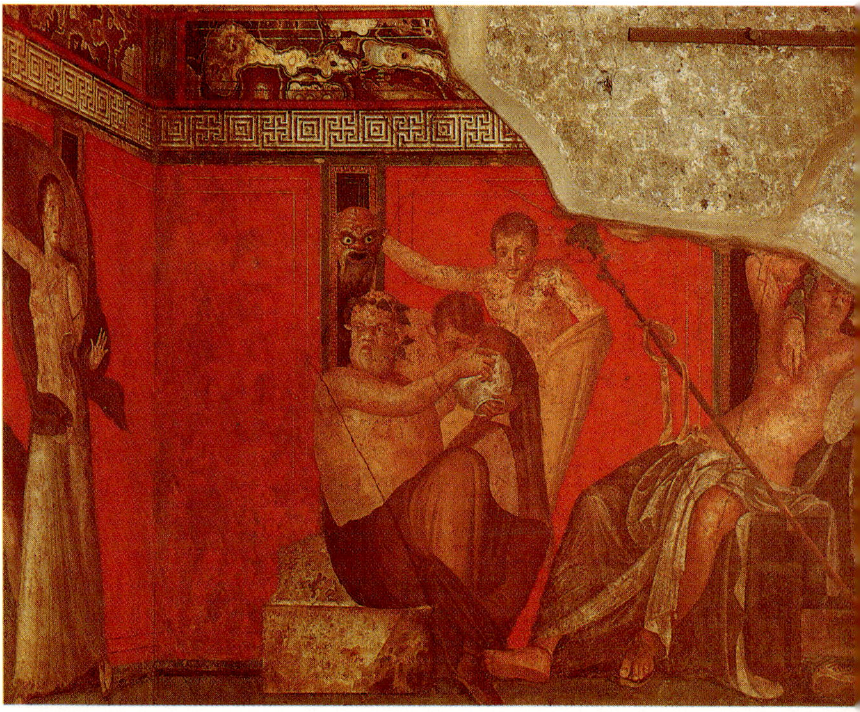

Scene 4 — Scene 5 — Scene 6

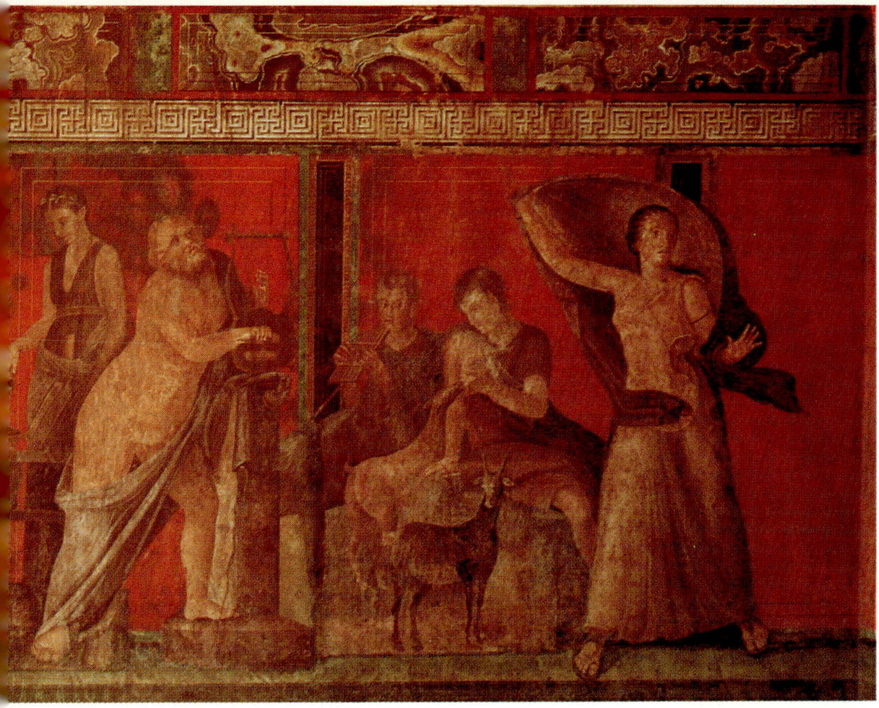

Scene 3 — Scene 4

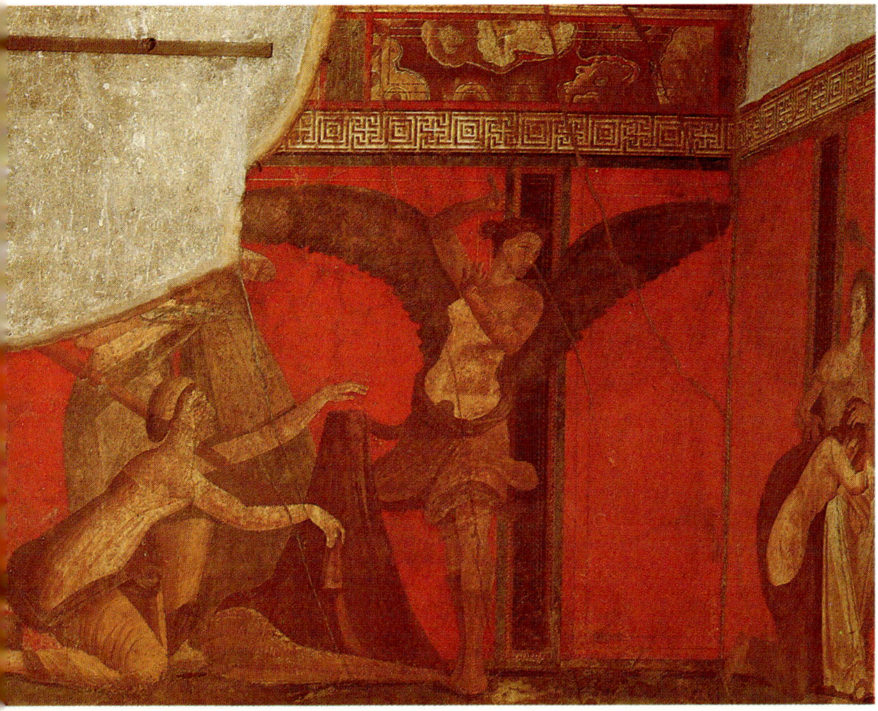

Scene 7 — Scene 8

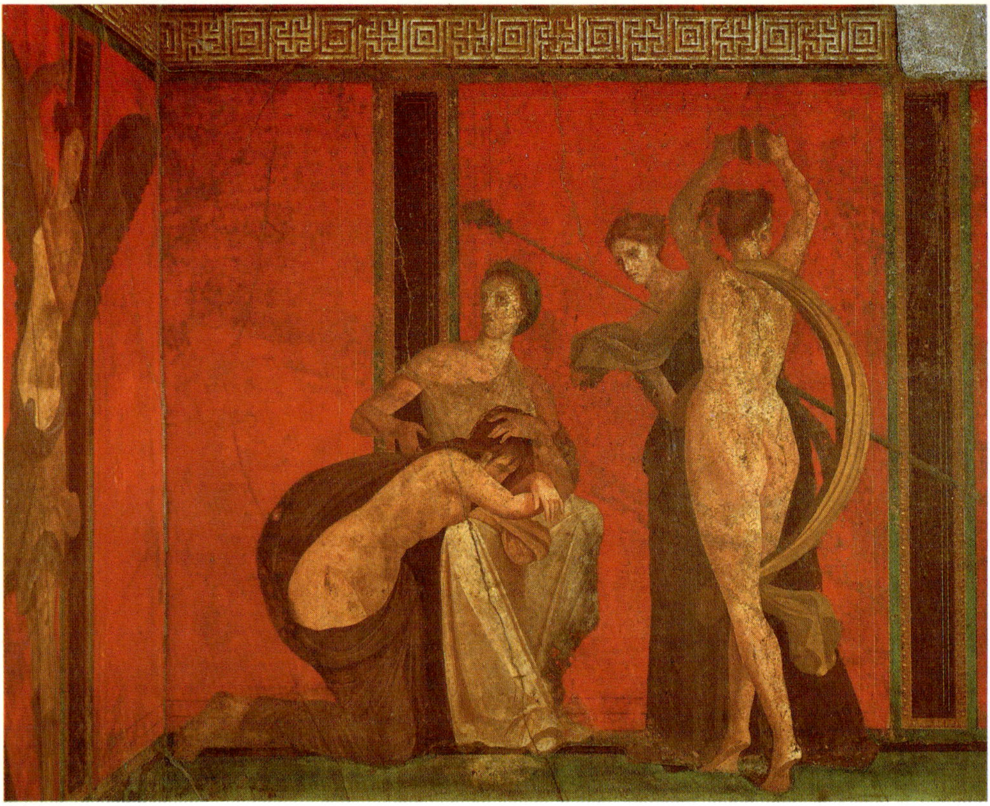

Scene 8

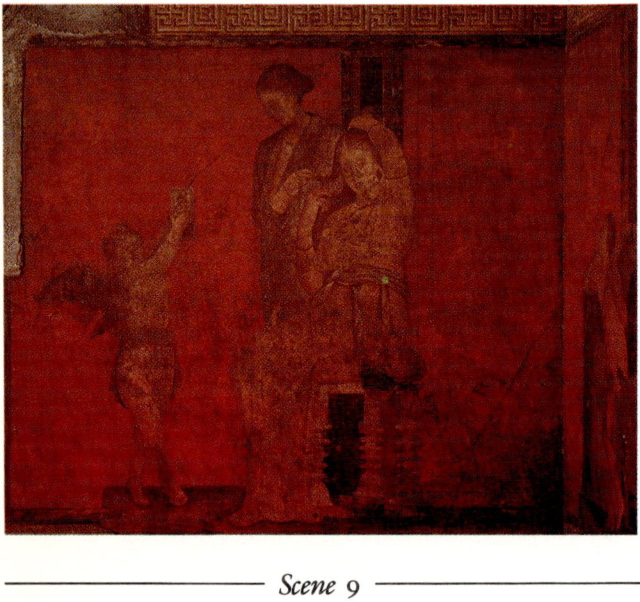

Scene 9

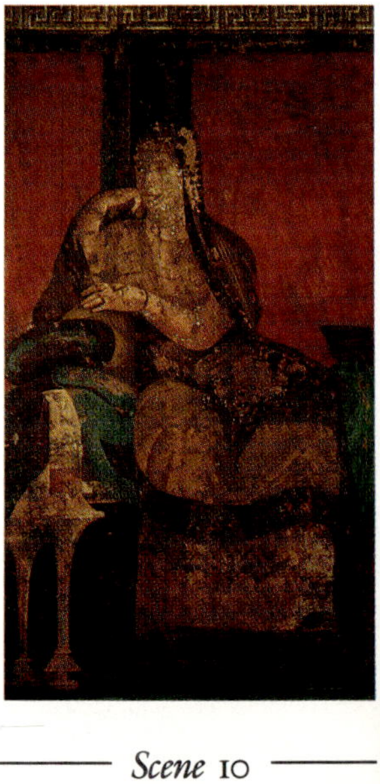

Scene 10

human being can never acquire for himself. In alchemy too this realization is a guiding principle, as it is also in Indian Yoga. *How* the wisdom is carried by tradition – that, indeed, can be entirely different from one case to another.

Orpheus taught while he sang and played the lyre, and his singing was so powerful that it mastered all nature. When he sang to his lyre, the birds flew around him, the fish left the water and sprang to him. The wind and the sea became still; the rivers flowed upward toward him. It did not snow and there was no hail. Trees and the very stones followed after Orpheus; tiger and lion lay near him next to the sheep, and the wolves next to the stag and roe. Now what does this mean? It surely means that through a divining insight into the meaning of natural events – through a discovery of meaningful progression in natural events, a *development,* like a series of costly divine statues – these events become harmoniously ordered from within. Everything becomes light and all creatures are appeased when the mediator, worshiping, reveals the light of nature. Orpheus is an embodiment of devotion and piety; he symbolizes the *religious attitude* that solves all conflict, since through this attitude the whole soul is turned toward that which lies on the other side of conflict. He is entirely surrender, entirely receptacle, entirely instrument of meaning. This is expressed in the ecstasy of the Silenus figure of our fresco. One might say he sings what the lyre plays by itself. And as he does this, he is truly an Orpheus, that is, a good shepherd, of which Orpheus was indeed a primitive embodiment. As Good Shepherd, at this level of the initiation, he guards the participants of our cult, for whom the attitude of this mediator serves as an example.

But one might remark that the participants in the mystery are not represented in this scene. The initiate too, whom we have seen in the two previous scenes, has disappeared. Instead of the human beings, we see a young faun, a panisk and three young goats near Silenus. The little faun-like pair are seated upon a small rock; the faun in the background plays a pastoral pipe, and a little kid leans against him. The panisk in front of him suckles a second kid, while a young buck stands attentively in the foreground looking out at us and listening, as though he were awaiting something.

Faun and panisk are surely symbols of that friendly-demonic light, visibly arising in previously dark and troubled nature as in a sunrise. The fauns are the sparks of Dionysus scattered in nature. Male fauns are often pictured with little snakes as phalluses, and they are always frighteningly wild or provocative, like the god. Nevertheless, in our picture even they seemed tamed by the song of Silenus. The male faun is characterized by the pastoral pipe. This is really the instrument of Pan, who in the old Orphic cult embodied the light of nature. An Orphic hymn glorifies him in these words:

> Freund der gottbegeisterten Seelen,
> Verzückter, wohnend in Höhlen,
> du spielst die Weltharmonie
> mit scherzendem Flötengesang . . .
> weidend der Menschen Geschlecht
> über dem unermesslichen Erdreich.[21]

> Friend of souls inspired by the god
> Enraptured one, living in caverns,
> Thou playest the harmony of the world
> with jesting song of the flute . . .
> tending the race of men
> over the immeasurable earth.

The same thing that Silenus has already symbolized is represented again at a deeper level in the young faun and his flute. Silenus's music disseminates itself into forest and field – the realm of the faun – and even the animal instills itself into the cosmic harmony. In connection with the panisk then, one can think of the nymphs who were the wet-nurses of Dionysus and danced with Pan upon the mountains. In these nymphs we have again the same idea which we have already met in the rude, archaic form of the Kordax dance, but in a milder and more poetic form: it is the changing dance of natural events. The panisk corresponds to these nymphs, for she too is a wet-nurse. At the same time, an aspect of Silenus is again sounded in her, on a deeper level, nearer the earth, for she too has a costly thing in her: sweet, nourishing milk. It is a deep and meaningful thought that rises with this symbolism, namely, that the light of nature – or the meaning which manifests itself in things themselves – is as nourishing as mother's milk. (At least in passing, I should like to mention a corresponding symbol in alchemy – the virgin's milk, *lac virginis.*) Everything that Silenus embodies realizes itself in the creatures that he, as Good Shepherd, guards: the wild and terrible are tamed; chaos becomes singing order; the holy water wells up and flows into the creatures as nourishing milk.

Luckily, we know exactly what kind of creatures little kids are, and so we can also answer the question,"What has become of the initiates?" This has come down to us from Orphic sources: it is the participants in the mystery who appear as little kids.

The symbol of the mystery participants as kids was of decisive importance in the Orphic cult. In graves, gold lozenges with inscriptions have been found, which the Orphics gave to their dead devotees to help them on their difficult way through the underworld. The inscriptions were supposed to awaken in the dead the memory of what they had experienced in the cult, which could also guide them after death and was their proof of identity before the ruler of souls, Dionysus. One small gold plate, found in a grave near Thurii, bears this inscription: "A god becamest thou from a human; a little kid, thou fellest in the milk."[22] This means that the dead should ponder that in life they already accomplished the way of transformation. In the animal form of the little kid or the little buck, they were already twice-born and immortal. They had accomplished the same transformation as Dionysus; and through this, the milk of Gnosis, of enlightenment, had become theirs to share. There are other gold lozenges whose inscriptions have the same meaning. The fall from human into animal – which is, however, at the same time divine – is, accordingly, the decisive step in the Orphic mystery cult: it is the prerequisite for redemption.

In our series of frescoes, when the initiate suddenly appears as a little kid one realizes that between the second and the third scene she has accomplished this change. Her former human shape had indeed not been human in the proper sense of the word; it had been determined by chaotic Titan nature. In the beginning, the initiate had been only "that personality which is split up into partial aspects, that bundle of odds and ends which *also* calls itself 'man'" as Jung said in the aforementioned passage from *Psychology and Alchemy.* To rediscover the primeval guiltlessness of pure animal nature means a decisive step forward in development, although experientially it must certainly first be felt as a fall.

After all, consider what the initiate undergoes when she becomes a little kid. As an animal she is deprived of human speech; she can no longer say what she feels, what happens in her. The loss of speech is almost like a death. How would it be in our hearts if we could still only bleat? This is truly a condition which can befall any of us: for example, when we suffer a shock. There are colloquial expressions such as "I am speechless" or "I have lost my tongue." These show very well what the fall into animal form in our mystery cult means in reality. The initiate has become as though thunderstruck and speechless.

This is how the first union of the participant with Dionysus looks – like a shock that entirely robs her of her tongue. Psychologically, this signifies a decisive loss of consciousness. When we have been struck by thunder, what we previously knew is no longer at our disposal and our good sense is to no avail. We are thereby removed to that entirely "other," irrational level of experience which corresponds with the symbolism of the fauns and the little animals in the rocky, fairytale forest.

The first change in the mystery cult is, therefore, loss of former consciousness. The participant becomes overpowered by occurrences which she cannot grasp. According to Orphic understanding, it is essential that human beings attain this condition. By just this experience, they become divinely branded for life, and even beyond death. By just this experience, they can legitimize themselves before the Ruler of Souls. They may say, "We have attained the threshold where the usual human consciousness is no longer anything and is no longer valid; we became little kids." The little kid in this sense is the symbol of the complete, dumb surrender of the human being to the Higher, which in the third scene of our fresco series appears embodied in Silenus-Orpheus.

A corresponding change is also characteristic for the individuation process of modern people. At the approach of powerful forces of the collective unconscious, we too suffer a shock that leads to a serious loss of consciousness. We too thereby become as little "kids." Modern people must realize that all our knowledge and ability fail in the face of occurrences which vastly surpass our capacities for consciousness, so that unreserved surrender is the only thing that remains. An inkling that this condition is approaching can express itself in symbols very similar to those we see in the third fresco scene. The ninth dream of the modern dreamer in chapter 2 of *Psychology and Alchemy* contains, for example, a short image that corresponds exactly: "A green land where many sheep are pastured. It is the 'land of sheep.'" C. G. Jung comments:

> This curious fragment, inscrutable at first glance, may derive from childhood impressions and particularly from those of a religious nature, which would not be far to seek in this connection – e.g., "He maketh me to lie down in green pastures," or the early Christian allegories of sheep and shepherd.[23]

As to the difference between the Christian symbolism of the sheep and the Dionysian of the little kid, one might briefly state the following: in the Christian symbol of the sheep, the light – tenderness, good will, harmlessness – is emphasized, whereas in the little kid, the dark – combativeness of sex, being faun-like – stands in the foreground. The acquiescent sheep embodies the obedient accessibility to wisdom and intelligence which has been given to the natural human being; the inquisitive goat embodies the equally natural tendency to allow oneself to be fascinated by the unknown and irrational. The latter is quite clearly represented by the young buck which, at the very front of the picture, looks and listens so intently for something that cannot yet be seen. As young animals which need a Good Shepherd, both sheep and goat stand for the early childhood condition, where human beings are still entirely and artlessly themselves. The fall into animal form is also a return to pure childlikeness, where the instincts still rule uncorrupted and the spirit is still free from the falsifications of civilization. The human being has been led back to a starting point, which he had to leave as he grew up. The green land of the sheep in the modern dream, the forest land of the fauns in the fresco are both symbols of the unconscious. Now the human being has reached it again; it sings to him and nourishes him; he can again nestle like a child against his mother's breast. Like a child, he can again hope for an unknown, new life.

But all this is only possible under the guidance of the Good Shepherd. If he were not there in the holy place, the human being would simply drown in the unconscious, and the outcome would be a regression into mere unconsciousness. The Good Shepherd shows the human being the light that is contained within the unconscious and points out the direction, while he holds the lyre and sings.

The myth says that Orpheus's lyre was removed to Heaven as a constellation of stars, which even today we designate with this name. The lyre, then, is a symbol like the crown of Ariadne, of which we spoke earlier. It also symbolizes the Self of the human being that was always there unconsciously, but now becomes conscious and appears above as a visible *goal*. In that the lyre represents the goal of the mystery way, it simultaneously stands for Dionysus himself, to whose figure, indeed, the music essentially belongs. The lyre symbolizes both the way to the goal and the goal itself. This fits psychologically also, for the goal becomes visible to human beings only through their particular way of individuation.

In our symbolism, the way and goal are characterized in the third scene through the tender, chirping tone of the old stringed instrument, which perhaps most nearly resembles a bird song. This tender tone, the alluring voice that sounds up from the unconscious and announces the Self, can be heard only *when the human being does not speak*. The lyre with its chirping tone is the *central symbol* in the third scene. Everything is related to it, and through it all beings are also related with one another. Music has the attribute that, while carried invisibly through the room, it binds together through its vibrations that which has been put asunder. In the third scene, music establishes the subtle relationship which unites Silenus with the fauns, and these figures again with the little animals. The initiate, who at the beginning of the initiation was isolated through the loss of her world – a forsaken woman like Ariadne – finds again a connection in which the uniting thing is entirely impersonal: the central symbol. When Silenus turns toward the lyre and, in ecstasy, causes it to sound, all creatures come into harmony, and everything is permeated with divine inspiration.

All this reminds one of the thirty-fifth verse of the *Tao-Teh-King* to which Richard Wilhelm gives the title "Das Leben der Liebe" (The Life of Love):

> Wer festhält das grosse Urbild, (das ist der Silen)
> zu dem kommt die Welt.
> Sie dommt und wird nicht verletzt,
> in Ruhe, Gleichheit und Seligkeit.
> Musik und Köder:
> Sie machen wohl den Wanderer auf seinem Wege anhalte.
> Der *Sinn* geht aus dem Munde hervor
> milde und ohne Geschmack.
> Du blickst nach ihm und siehst nichts Sonderliches,
> Du hörst nach ihm und hörst nichts Sonderliches.
> Du handelst nach ihm und – findest kein Ende.
>
> Whoever holds fast the great archetype, (That is Silenus)
> to him the world comes.
> It comes and is not wounded,
> in peace, in equality and in bliss.
> Music and enticement:
> Indeed, they make the wanderer pause upon his way.
> *Meaning* comes forth from the mouth
> mild and without flavor.
> Thou glancest at him and seest nothing remarkable.
> Thou listenest to him and hearest nothing remarkable.
> Thou reachest toward him and – findest no end.

We come now to still another entirely different aspect of the third scene, that is, to the question of whether or not the pictured representation asserts something about the *practice* of the mystery cult. The question is justified, for both of the first scenes point out how the initiation was actually practiced. Since we know that the little kids signify initiates, it has been suggested by Feiler, among others, that the fauns and Silenus might also represent higher grades of initiation. This is probable insofar as the meaning of a priestly guide is already included in the symbolism of Silenus. This belongs to his human side; among other things he is the embodiment of a Mana personality, as we might say. Also, the Silenus figure on our fresco clearly bears Socratic features. He has the broad, flat face and the pressed-in nose, as Socrates is portrayed. This must concern a conscious allusion: a superior teacher was indicated, a wise man like the Platonic Socrates. Naturally, we cannot know whether at this level of initiation an Orphic high priest, for example, and higher participants under him may have collaborated in the initiation. We can only say that the pictured representation does not speak against it. Besides, it has a certain psychological probability.

As I said in the introduction, the cultivated Roman woman was consciously related most directly to the man (and not to the child). For this reason, perhaps she needed the spiritual guidance of a superior masculine personality, "Socrates," on the mystery way in order to arrive at a spirituality of her own. In general, also, what is a woman without a man? The sexes need one another on every level. Especially concerning their *spiritual* development, women are dependent on men. In the first place, they receive spiritual instruction through the fathers and through the men in their circle of life. These mediate knowledge, which every individual woman – each according to her capacity – takes up and uses for herself.

The medium of this transmission is speech, in which the entire spiritual tradition is contained and which, to a very large extent, an individual uses in order to think. Certainly no man alone can think through everything about which he glibly speaks. It is the same for all human beings, but with women there is a particular complication. For them, the spirit – like everything masculine – belongs to the contents of the unconscious and appears as an *image*. Because they cannot deal with it consciously, it has the autonomous character of a demon or a ghost. C. G. Jung calls this extraordinarily potent archetypal image the animus. Above all, however, women experience this image in projection: it comes to meet them from the fathers and the men in their circle; it colors too the knowledge that is conveyed to them from these men. Therefore, spiritual wealth, which is handed down through speech, has an impressive mystery for women.

Everything they know has a psychic value also; the image of the animus manifests itself in it and leads them on, so that under certain circumstances they are intensely involved with words, especially if they do not rightly understand them. In a peculiar way, words can be important and incontrovertibly true for women because they can contain a psychic reality – precisely the image of the animus, which properly belongs to women themselves and also expresses their own spirituality. Therefore on the one hand, women regard meaningful words lightly, as their possession; and on the other hand, they hypostatize (or give literal substance to) them. That is, when they say, for example, "Spirit," or "the Good," or "Justice," they often unintentionally give substantiality to these abstract concepts as though they were things which belong to someone, things which he could put in his pocket.

What I describe here is what one today calls the *animus opinions* of women. All grown women who have a certain level of education – however this may have been procured – have their pockets full of animus opinions. As soon as these are called into question, they build these opinions around themselves like a solid ivory tower, in which they then sit, unassailably safe. One often meets this phenomenon today in the field of psychology with its attractive new formulation of ideas. There are many women who throw psychological terms at other people with the greatest assurance, as though with the idea they had placed a real thing, something about which one can say: *est, est* – it *is*. They entrench themselves behind such concretized abstractions, producing not only an ivory tower but also a whole bastion with mounted guns.

For other people this can be utterly irritating; for the women themselves it is painful, even grievous. Somewhere in their innermost selves, they know quite certainly that with the words they do not possess the reality of the demonic image, that, rather, it possesses them, makes a fool of them with concepts and principles, in order always to escape them again. The fire with which women can defend their animus opinions originates in the deep insecurity in which they are suspended in relation to the reality of the basic image. They build ever higher a self-made ivory tower of Solomon-like wisdom basically only because they long for true guidance and for their own spirituality; they continue to hope that they will find them in the end.

For the Roman women of Hellenic times, it was not much different. The world of ideas was a somewhat more mythical-philosophical world, but its effect on women was similar. We only need look at the first women's figures of the Pompeiian fresco series in order to realize this. The initiate of the first scene does enter the chamber with correct modesty but, at the same time, with a sure bearing that allows no doubt as to her competence to handle what is to happen. She is a little ivory tower in person, entirely unassailable. The woman who carries the sacrificial cake and is already puffed up with a Dionysian frame of mind still has this same, self-assured bearing. Think also of the statue of Livia, found in the Villa of Mysteries. She too is an ivory tower of Solomon-like wisdom. Many portrait-statues and busts of Roman ladies are in their expressions very like the prominent women today.

This first development of women – their animus-like absorption in the intellectual domain of men, whether pleasant or not – is still the necessary premise for the inner development to come. Through this development, the archetypal image of the animus becomes more vividly, more pressingly constellated. If women then succeed in turning their backs to the world, if they start upon the "mystery way" and become speechless before the breath of the collective unconscious, then through this first step they are freed from animus opinions. They are released from the magic of words. The archetypal image of the animus as *leader of souls* is freed also from its previous cloak: it stands visible, in our fresco series, as the Orphic Silenus, a mother-father and wise teacher, such as never exists in reality. This figure may, nevertheless, have first appeared to these women perhaps through a priestly man as bearer of the archetypal image.

A woman must first experience spiritual things that are unconscious through an appropriate man. So perhaps these Roman women of the Pompeiian private cult, whose consciousness failed before the approach of the divine, also needed a real guide, someone like Socrates, who could not only put their heads right, in the true sense of the expression, but also teach them how the ineffable mystery of the psyche can be religiously received. Perhaps they needed a real Good Shepherd who tamed and lovingly accepted everything that had remained childishly undeveloped in them – or even what was subhuman, like an animal. No person can accept his weakness and helplessness if he has not been accepted by another who has authority. For a woman, the "Socratic" teacher, who is for her a Mana personality, has this authority. Through him, she establishes a new connection with those persons who have gathered around him and who through him are all related in the same way to a central symbol.

Such communities have always existed. The problem of speechlessness and helplessness sinks into nothing as soon as one experiences how everyone is helpless before the divine. This new sense of harmony rests on the fundamental need of all human beings for help. The medium through which the harmony is established can no longer be speech or learning. In the Orphic cult, harmony is realized through the symbol of music. Music was and is the essential expression of *feeling* that, without touching the head, can go directly to the heart and break forth from it. The lyre of Orpheus, of course, does not symbolize outer music which one can set to notes and play on real instruments or sing, but an inner music. Richard Wilhelm in the title of the thirty-fifth verse of the *Tao-Teh-King* called it the *life of love*. The third scene of our fresco series is so peaceful and lovely because it represents for this cult the experience of love, that which reaches through all human spheres even to the divine and binds all things together.

If the psychological interpretation that I have tried to give to these fresco representations is correct, we might draw the interesting conclusion that a woman's own spirit is first awakened through love of the super-personal. Accordingly, a religious character must be characteristic of the feminine spirit. It can first unfold when all words and all outer music are silent and the "inner" music of love sounds. Then the spirit of women frees itself from a chrysalis state and becomes visible as it really looks when the ivory tower of opinions crumbles: still subhuman and itself still dumb. In the third fresco scene this state is symbolized by the *little buck* in the foreground of the picture – by this impatient, aggressive little animal. It had previously colored the animus opinions of the women with its demonic heat. Meanwhile, it has clearly fallen into the milk; it has cooled off and gazes now in a new direction: no longer into the world, but into the unknown future. It is ready to spring.

The Fourth and Fifth Scenes

The fourth scene is dramatically stirring. We must discuss this scene in connection with the fifth, for these two belong together in meaning, although Maiuri has numbered them separately. To be sure, Maiuri has good grounds. After the figure of the so-called terrified woman, the only figure of the fourth scene, the first long wall of the Initiation Hall comes to an end, so this woman's picture seems to form an entire scene by itself. What comes later stands behind the woman, so to speak, on the short wall of the chamber, whose middle piece is the large picture of Dionysus and Ariadne. I stated earlier that the image of the god and his beloved must be thought of as *invisibly* present. But the proceedings which are represented on the short back wall of the chamber also have something uncommon about them. They illustrate things which take place in close proximity to the god, in an inner sanctuary. The so-called terrified woman has not yet reached this innermost sphere. She finds herself still in the vestibule, as it were, still in the outer sanctuary where the first three scenes were enacted. I use the terms "inner" and "outer" sanctuary here only in the sense of an "as if" and only to make it clear that the various walls reflect various spheres of the cult. What is portrayed on the short wall has, at any rate, the character of a "Holy of Holies" or an *anaktoron*. Whoever is within can gaze out from there, but no one can look in. Its significance will surely become understandable if we describe the events of the fourth scene in connection with the fifth.

The first figure, as we said, is the agitated figure of a woman who gazes forward with open lips, as though she would utter a cry. She has stretched out her left hand as though warding something off, and her body is engaged in striding vehemently in the direction from which she has come. With her right hand she has seized her cloak in order to throw it over her head. Her step is so rapid that her cloak billows out over her. On the short wall behind her, we see again the Silenus of the third scene. He sits on a four-sided hewn stone; a dark, wine-red cloak now covers the entire lower half of his body, and his head is crowned with ivy. He looks back toward the terrified woman and listens attentively as though asking himself, "What will she do now?" His features are again pronouncedly Socratic, but the expression of his face is no longer ecstatic, but wise and stern. While he glances back, he leans forward and lifts a silver receptacle shoulder-high. A young faun behind him bends over this receptacle and raises his eyebrows in terror. A second young faun, who stands behind the first, smiles slyly at the onlooker. At the same time, he raises a gloomy, threatening satyr-mask such as was used in Greek theater; he raises it so high that it appears to be immediately behind the head of Silenus.

What sort of a drama is this? One naturally asks oneself what might have driven the so-called terrified woman into a flight backward. She is not represented as though she could see the frightful mask. Maiuri, who is always very careful in his descriptions, therefore tries to follow the direction of her glance. To him her glance appeared to be turned toward the scene of the flagellation, so perhaps her terror reflects a presentiment of the coming torture.

For the moment, we will put this question aside and turn toward the religious proceedings being consummated behind the "terrified" woman. That this takes place in an innermost sanctuary is indicated by the four-sided hewn stone on which Silenus sits. Just as the rough stone in the third scene indicated the rocky forest of the fauns, so the hewn stone here indicates the *anaktoron* of a temple. The proceedings also have the character of a divine service. What happens is this: two objects are elevated. One is the silver receptacle that must hold wine. This is indicated by the wine-red cloak of Silenus and also by his crown of ivy. The ivy belongs to Dionysus as god of wine. The other object that is elevated is the terrible mask which belongs to Dionysus as ruler of the underworld. I will come back to this later. Both objects are, at any rate, Dionysian symbols; to elevate them is a ritualistic gesture which signifies that in these, his symbols, the god is invoked. The elevation of the religious symbol is a primitive, holy gesture which is supposed to invoke the *epiphany* of the god. It calls the god, that he may fill the elevated religious objects and so may be present for the faithful.

In this regard, I refer to what C. G. Jung says in his essay "Transformation Symbolism in the Mass" about the elevation of the chalice:

> The lifting up of the chalice in the air prepares the spiritualization (i.e., volatilization) of the wine. This is confirmed by the invocation to the Holy Ghost which immediately follows (*Veni sanctificator*), and it is even more evident in the Mozarabic liturgy, which has "Veni spiritus sanctificator." The invocation serves to infuse the wine with holy spirit, for it is the Holy Ghost who begets, fulfils, and transforms. . . .[24]

The ritual gestures of the cults are an archetypal treasure; their meaning is universal. The elevation of the Dionysian wine receptacle is also an act of invocation of the spirit, which may beget, fulfill, and transform. The spirit, nevertheless, is also present in archaic, gloomy form in the mask of terror.

To understand this, we must turn to the cult of Dionysus in Delphi, where the idea of the epiphany plays a special role. We must go somewhat more closely into this cult. In Delphi, Apollo, the summer sun, and Dionysus, the winter sun – these irreconcilable opposites – were reconciled, and we shall see later how extraordinarily important this reconciliation is for the meaning of the fifth scene. Both gods were venerated alternately in the same Delphic temple, Apollo in the summer and Dionysus in the cold wintertime.

The Delphic temple also contained the grave of Dionysus in the form of a step cut into rock; that is, he was present there chiefly as a dead person or a spirit of the dead. As such he bore also the name *Isodaites* (exact divider), that is, he who invites all people to himself in the same way. As Apollo at Delphi was life, so Dionysus was death and the god of death. It was believed that as long as he rested in the grave, he sojourned in the underworld house of Persephone among the souls and spirits of the dead, whose master he was. However, every second year his return was celebrated in great nocturnal festivals, about which, for example, Erwin Rohde has written with much understanding in his book *Psyche.*[25] Comparatively speaking, there is a good deal known about these celebrations; they were much discussed because a delegation of Athenian matrons always took part in them. The sequence of the celebrations was a very remarkable one. An epiphany of Dionysus in the form of an aural event formed the introduction. One heard him bellow as the invisible bull-god; the so-called mimes of terror allowed one to feel the presence of the invisible god through the simulated bellowing of bulls. The women were aroused into an orgiastic, nocturnal procession to wake the dead and bring home the resurrected god as a small child in the winnowing basket. During this procession, the priests of Apollo held a mystery service in the temple of Delphi. So it is that the god himself, appearing in the bellowing of a bull, announces his return and awakens the faithful so they will awaken him. As we have already explained in the scene of the sacrament, the sacrificed god is at the same time also the sacrificer, the devoured also the devourer. So it is here also: when the god is awakened, he is himself the awakener.

In the nocturnal procession at Delphi, the matrons appeared as nurses of Dionysus. They were called *Thyiades* (the violent ones), for they rushed impetuously out, swinging torches, to fetch the god. The place of his return was the Korykian Cave on Parnassus, the mountain of Apollo. According to legends, a golden light issued from this cave from time to time which announced the divine child. Whether the Delphic Thyiades really dashed up as far as the Korykian Cave is not known. But there are legends which tell how they ran almost senselessly, with unbelievable speed, so that individuals went astray and had to be brought home again from a great distance. Although dignified matrons played the role of Thyiades, they nevertheless behaved with Dionysian frenzy. They were full of the god; and so, filled with him, they became his nurses. We have here again the same feature as before: as the god is nourished, he is himself the nourisher.

During the procession of women, the priests of Apollo celebrated a mystery service in the temple at Delphi, as we have already said. Accordingly, men and women celebrated the return of the god in common, but at the same time they were separated and only the women fell into a frenzy. The women returned with the winnowing basket, carrying the divine child into the Delphic temple. This symbol of the *winnowing basket* became an important attribute of the god in the private Orphic cults of southern Italy. A winnowing basket or a basket with fruits was used by the Orphics in the cult. Under the fruits which filled the basket, Dionysus was believed to be hidden in the form of a phallus. We will speak of this symbolism more fully when we consider the seventh scene.

In other mythical parallels too, the approach of the god as a divine, bellowing bull signifies the call to the women to arouse themselves and seek the god in a violent rush. There are also various legends which show what happens if the women do *not* follow the call. It is told of the daughters of Minyas of Orchomenus and the daughters of Proitos of Sikyon that they refused to follow the divine Dionysian call. They preferred to stay home in the clear Apollonian daylight. The same is told of Pentheus's mother. Dionysus punished all these women with madness so that, in a blind rage, they killed their own children. When women obey the call of the god, he leads them to divinely wild activity, from which life comes forth. If they oppose him and remain passive, they become deadly. For the divine caller *is* indeed death: just as Heraclitus said, "It is Hades for whom they rave and celebrate feasts." So when he approaches, there is only one alternative: either the women give themselves up to the god in holy frenzy, or death is disseminated in their neighborhood. The women can propitiate the ruler of souls and the spirits of the dead only when they themselves rush toward his deadly, ghostly breath, so that through them his warm, living, creative power (the phallus in the basket) can be renewed. They must actively make themselves vehicles for the transformation from death to life.

According to the old myths of Dionysus and also the winter celebrations in Delphi, only women have this task. Men do not. In Delphi the men celebrated in the privacy of the temple of Apollo, while the women rushed away from it, and something like this appears in the fourth and fifth fresco scenes of the Pompeiian Initiation Chamber. It seems to me, at least, that one could understand the meaning of these two scenes in connection with these patterns of cult and myth which I have just cited.

At the time I saw the frescoes in the Villa of Mysteries, the movement of the so-called terrified woman made a great impression immediately. But it was not her terror that struck me most, but the remarkable way she seems to *spring out* of the frame of the fresco. It looks as though she does not simply run back, but rather begins to spring down out of the frieze and directly into the Initiation Hall. One foot is already out of the frame as though she meant to run away through the hall. The riddle of this stormy, terrified movement was first solved for me through parallels with the Delphic awakening festivals. If one regards the fourth and fifth scenes from this point of view, everything fits. The so-called terrified woman is the initiate who has again received human form. The love idyll of the third scene, in which she had dissolved, is at an end; passive surrender no longer suffices. The human form, which she has again acquired, shows that she *has come to herself.* Then she becomes frightened, but not about something that she sees. She is frightened by the call of the mask of terror that comes resounding out of the innermost sanctuary. She throws her cloak around her: already she has become a Thyiad. It is as Dionysian nurse that she rushes away to awaken the divine child. The correctness of this interpretation is established by the representation in the seventh scene, for there the Thyiad actually comes back with a torch, bringing the winnowing basket with the phallus in it. The fifth scene, which is enacted between Silenus and the two fauns, must in this case correspond in meaning to the mystery service of the priests of Apollo which is going on at the same time in the temple at Delphi. Silenus, as celebrating priest, elevates the receptacle of wine, after one of the young fauns has officiated as "Mime of Terror." Or is it he? Did Silenus himself wear the mask of terror? Did he himself arouse the initiate with a frightful call? This, one does not know. But at all events, the young faun in the background is represented with such a sly expression on his face because he knows that *nothing* is behind the mask.

Like all the other details of these frescoes, this too must be understood symbolically. The mask behind which there is nothing belongs, of course, precisely to the cult of Dionysus. There are old

Greek illustrations which show this idea. They depict a pillar, rough or hewn four-square, with a drapery around it, and under one capital is only the bearded mask of Dionysus. There is nothing behind it. Vase pictures too have been preserved which represent religious ceremonies of women in the temple, over whom no image of the god hangs, but only an empty mask.[26] The "nothing" behind the mask is Dionysus as spirit of the dead, that is, as embodiment of a spirit that does not live under the sun of consciousness, but in the gloom of the unconscious. Thus the Sanctifier of our Orphic frescoes is Dionysus as spirit of the unconscious, which "begets, fulfills and transforms." For further reference we can read C. G. Jung's article on "The Spirit Mercurius" in *Alchemical Studies*.[27]

Mercurius as spirit and soul, like Mercurius in his antinomic, two-fold nature, corresponds directly with Dionysus as mask and wine. We may also remind ourselves that the holy water, which seems in our frescoes to be embodied in Silenus in the third scene, is also a symbol of the alchemical transformation substance; so we have a further parallel which is likewise cited in the same chapter of Jung's essay mentioned above. We shall speak later of other parallels. At any rate, we can hold to it in principle that the alchemical Mercurius represents an impressive parallel to the central symbol of our frescoes, even if – in order not to exceed the limits of this presentation – we cannot go into detail.

It is extraordinarily significant that in the Delphic festivals, as also in our frescoes in the fourth and fifth scenes, the central symbol of Dionysus is the same for men and women, namely, of his two-fold epiphany. But they react to it in entirely different ways. Women are overpowered by it, impelled to run impetuously away; men, in contrast, withdraw into the silence of the innermost holy place. What is done there appears to be indicated in the figure of the foremost young faun, who bends over the receptacle of wine. Maiuri, whose careful description is altogether reliable, has observed that this young faun is *not* represented as *drinking* wine. He only *gazes* into the receptacle. Maiuri further points out that, due to the way the young faun bends over, he must see the reflection of the Dionysian mask in the wine that he contemplates, and this is why his face expresses terror and stupefaction. This observation is meaningful, for the wine and the mask symbolize the same thing, namely, Dionysus as spirit-soul. In the wine, just as in the mask, he appears as the *Lysios* (loosener, deliverer) which begets, fulfills and transforms, as Jung said.

Let us consider once more the woman of the fourth scene. To throw a cloak over one's head is a ritual gesture of classical mystery cults. Covering the head during a mystery initiation signified the *death* of the initiate.[28] In the old Orphic mysteries, this death was represented very drastically. The participant was buried in the earth up to his head and left there until unconscious. He could not know in advance whether he would survive or descend unshriven into Hades. *At this moment everything hung in the balance.* I dare say it was the same for the initiate of our Orphic cult. Although she was not buried, she was nevertheless suddenly torn from the quiet pace of the initiation. The idyllic third scene had filled her with a presage of love and ecstasy. How could she have foreseen that the ecstasy would be so deadly! Perhaps this moment of the initiation also included a kind of test for the initiate. She was aroused and whether she would now behave rightly or not – perhaps this hung in the balance for her. The way the Silenus in the fifth scene looks after her is watchful, with a truly probing severity. Perhaps now all depended on whether the initiate would *run after* the voice of the god or whether she would *run away* frightened, breaking off the initiation.

While I thought back over this scene, I gave rein a little to my fancy. I imagined that the initiate really had to make a leap at this moment of the initiation, just as it is represented in the fresco – forward out of the chamber and downward! It occurred to me that around the front of the Villa of Mysteries runs a vaulted cellar way, the so-called Criptoportico. It is ninety-five meters (about one hundred yards) long, dark, and approachable from the north by a very narrow, steep staircase. On the south side, an almost equally narrow staircase leads up again. This cellar way is considered to have been a storeroom for agricultural products, but there was no sign of any such thing found in it. I asked myself whether perhaps a stormy procession might have gone through this long resounding passage. Well, this possibility is naturally only a fantasy of mine.[29]

Then I reflected on the striking fact that in the place of the initiation, which the fourth and fifth scenes represent, the experiences of men and women are entirely different. One can say outright: here the ways of the sexes part. This is psychologically noteworthy. For us today this is not a matter of course. Already it has become striking, for example, when men and women take seats on separate benches in church in the primitive way. Otherwise, too, there is hardly anything of importance that is not common to both men and women. What a man can do and be, today a woman can also do and be. Modern women have more than fulfilled the program of emancipation that Roman women exemplified two thousand years ago. Like them, only equipped with somewhat more modern weapons, we also sit in our bastions and ivory towers, very emancipated and impregnable.

There are two remarkable examples of emancipated Roman women in the New Testament, namely, Herodias and Salome. They were two very influential ladies who allowed a holy ascetic to be beheaded in cold blood because he threatened to disturb the fragile balance in the Roman provinces, two politicians to whom the human and the holy were a matter of indifference. Naturally, the poor fishermen in Palestine did not understand this. But they sensed what was behind these women: the wicked aggressiveness of the lion and the calculating coldness of the snake, whom no Good Shepherd had tamed and transformed into a little kid. For this reason, Herodias lived on even into the Middle Ages, together with Diana, as legendary leader of coveys of witches. The woman who saw and avenged guilt only in others had become successor to Medea. From a psychological point of view, this is absolutely correct; and it only shows how important it was, at that time, that mystery cults existed in which at least some women, following the example of Ariadne, could recognize their own guilt and throw themselves into the arms of the transformative death for which the spirit, as redeemer, could fulfill them.

But from a psychological standpoint, how is it to be understood that, according to this ancient view, the ways of men and women separate when Dionysus manifests himself as the spirit of the unconscious? Why must women, at this moment, hurl themselves so vehemently into death-like darkness while men draw back into the stillness of a sanctuary? To me these answers seem important, for somehow they concern the essence of all men and women. We will therefore try to see whether an answer can be found – above all in reference to women, who certainly stand in the foreground in our mystery cult.

Concerning the symbolism of the third scene, we discussed the first spiritual development of the women, thereby touching the phenomenon of animus opinions. This results in a one-sided picture of women, for we have not yet mentioned their other side, namely, their natural womanliness. In their womanliness, all women are conditioned by the principle of Eros or, more simply, by the principle of *relatedness*. They stretch out the feelers of relatedness and let themselves become enmeshed in people, things, and experiences. They mix themselves in everything not because they *want* to, but because from the beginning they have been mixed in everything that surrounds them; they have been tied to everything through their natural capacity for relatedness. Their life flows not only in themselves; it flows *between* them and all that stands near to them. Such is the nature of relatedness: a blending with a moon-like quality. This is why women build the walls of their opinions so high about them, because they hope to achieve a certain separateness from objects. But mere opinions naturally do not suffice; at most, the relatedness becomes negative.

The phenomenon of womanly relatedness is presented, for example, in the story of the three daughters of Minyas who did not want to follow Dionysus's deathly call. According to the tale, they preferred to stay at home at their weaver's looms. This is an excellent symbol for the Eros of women, which spins and weaves a thousand threads of relatedness in order to entangle and ensnare others; but nevertheless, in the end, the women themselves become the fettered ones. To live according to the principle of relatedness, to let oneself be entangled and to entangle others, is a necessity by nature for all women, and the more honorable they are at it, the better it is for them. But as soon as relatedness is carried on at the expense of one's own soul, as soon as women overflow too unreservedly into the surrounding world – and somewhere this happens to everyone – a powerful countercurrent arises in them. If it remains unconscious, it shows itself in a Maenad-like aggressiveness which kills in order to cut threads and break chains. This is sometimes represented in myths in which women kill their own children. Indeed, actual children are often lamed in their own lives or even killed through women's Maenad-like aggressiveness. But children also symbolize all that life which women have created through their natural relatedness, that life which in some circumstances suddenly falls victim to their own aggressiveness.

In their womanliness, women are completely turned toward *life*. Here they need new life, again and again, and still more life, because they can truly relate only to life. This is life of nature as well as life of the spirit. Indeed, we saw earlier how intensely women can relate to spiritual phenomena. But in the Dionysian epiphany, the spirit appears as death and as the summoning spirit realm. Over and against overburdened life, *death* reveals itself as the *highest value*. The bellowing of the ghostly bull-god heralds the frightful necessity of rending all ties in themselves and giving up all relatedness in the world, in order to find the relationship to the spirit and therewith also to themselves. Women must do this with the greatest vehemence. They must cover their heads like the terrified woman of the Villa of Mysteries and dare to make the leap into darkness. This vehemence is necessary because subduing the worldly Eros surely means the heaviest sacrifice for every naturally womanly woman. She loses so much that she seems to herself like a ghost among ghosts. At this moment of development, a great deal actually hangs in the balance for every woman with an inner life, and it is a test, for no woman can know in advance whether she will lose forever the life which flows from relatedness or whether she will remain ghost-like. Only the god-spirit knows.

For men everything seems to be different; for them the divine spirit manifests itself in *wine*. Women, in the cold breath of the spirit realm, experience also their own coldness, which counterbalances the warmth of relatedness; but in this same situation, Dionysus appears to men in the warm, genial fragrance of the "special juice." In it the terrified young faun contemplates the mask, behind which is nothing. When we reflect on how wine works on men, we can perhaps understand something of this symbolism. The man who is governed by the principle of Logos originally remains separate in the face of things, just as the sun illuminates the earth from afar. To be able to realize clearly and differentiate, he needs this separateness. Therefore, often it is precisely manly men who instinctively shrink from all entanglements, avoiding them wherever they can. Relatedness is something that happens to natural men rather than something they seek; and when it happens, they still hope it is not important. Often men can overcome their natural separateness only through conscious fidelity to the objects that do in fact surround them, but there is naturally a certain strain connected with this. Therefore, men value fidelity in the highest degree as a virtue. The animus preaches the same to women, for they in their womanliness have no need for conscious fidelity. In that respect they are as changeable as the moon – related to all earthly things, at first one way and then again differently. Therefore men accuse women of the vice of fickleness. For men themselves, of course, fickleness is negative in the utmost, since through it they remain caught in their natural separateness. (An illustrative example is Don Juan.)

But wine pulls men out of their separateness and mediates the experience of direct union. Through wine they find direct contact with other people and with the earth. For this reason the symposiums of men were so important in classical antiquity: they gave rise to friendships and furthered love relationships between older men and youths in whom at that time a masculine Eros was anchored. Through wine then, men achieved relatedness. The best example is Plato's *Symposium,* in which vigorous dialogue on everything flows. Wine, wisdom, inspired feeling – all is sustained by the most exquisite wantonness.

When, as appears in our cult, the wine is not drunk but is elevated and contemplated, the god-spirit may manifest himself. This action symbolizes that only *religious feeling* can educate men about real relatedness. Only in this sphere can they really give themselves into captivity and allow themselves to be ensnared. Even the Platonic Socrates allowed himself to be instructed on the nature of Eros only through the mysteriously remote priestess Diotima. The wine in the silver receptacle of our Orphic cult is a *feminine symbol* similar to the Holy Grail. With this mysteriously pulsating receptacle, Dionysus appears to men as the soul of inspiration or anima. This is for men a terrifying experience also, for now the man who was formerly free becomes a slave. One might quote here the definition which an alchemical master gave of Mercurius as soul, namely, that he is a "'life-giving power, which at the same time is like a glue, holding the world together and standing in the middle between body and spirit.'"[30]

While women leap from life into death at the approach of the divine spirit, men arrive in the intermediate realm of living relatedness through the death of their sun-like separateness. Whereas women remove themselves to a distance, men go "into the trap." For men then, just as much hangs in the balance as for women. They too cannot know whether the spectral vision of the receptacle, which holds them captive, will lead to real life or whether life will now become ghostly. Only the god-soul knows.

The representation of the fourth and fifth fresco scenes, which can be explained up to this point by the Delphic cult, contains still another hint in relation to *earthly* connections which appears noteworthy from a psychological standpoint. As we have seen, men hold their mystery service while the women are out on their orgiastic procession. This means that the women rush away *first,* and not until later do the men begin the divine service. This is a meaningful detail which accurately corresponds with real psychic circumstances. As long as men are chained by the intense relatedness of women and bound to them, they are involuntarily held fast in their natural separateness. For as long as women are the bound and binding, the business of separating and deciding is necessarily laid upon men. They must grasp the initiative again and again in order to hold separate everything interwoven and entangled. Therefore, men usually hold the active and decisive positions in the world. Here they take the initiative. Women do not need this position in the world; without it, they have a part in everything through relatedness. In relation to *inner* development, however, women take the initiative. Here they first of all must be active; they must cast themselves into the arms of the deathly savior spirit, that he may deliver them from the compulsion of a relatedness that is in thrall to nature. Then for the first time, men have the freedom to turn to their own most particular mystery service and to take upon themselves the Dionysian fetters that also deliver them.

These very same psychic conditions exist today, as they did in the time of the Roman Empire. Modern women, indeed, are just as emancipated as Roman women. Therefore, just like the women of Rome, the cultivated modern women during the course of life arrive at a boundary where outer striving with men, in the sense of claiming masculine initiative, loses all value. Then a deathly breath brushes them, and *nolens volens* they are likewise set free from their worldly relatedness. Many modern women sense this instinctively. At any rate, it is no accident that women, above all, are interested in psychological work today. For them the search into the contents of the unconscious is of primary importance. In this field women must take the initiative; they must – each according to her lot – even hurl themselves upon it. Then the life of the world, at least in the individual sphere, is relieved of confusion and entanglement, and men need no longer only drink the delicious juice of the wine. They can meditate in quiet upon the "life-giving power" in the receptacle which "is like a glue . . . between body and spirit." Through this then, in the case of men too, excessive activity which pours itself unbearably into events of the world is dammed and alleviated in a salutary way.

The bellowing of the spirit bull is a symbol that is not without meaning for modern people also. Today, as we all know, our world is filled with a deadly breath. We stand under the Damocles sword of mass-murder and world-wide, terrible destruction. Perhaps we could most easily bear the bellowing of death that presses upon us from all sides if we understood it in the sense of a Dionysian call to awakening, if we saw that the arousing spirit urges us to awaken him. Even though our manner of expression is no longer the same, even though we describe Dionysus-Hades as the spirit of the unconscious, the basic psychic facts are at least similar to those in Hellenic times. Like ancient people, we see not only our personal property or our personal luck threatened with destruction. We see our whole culture and all our conscious values stagger. We experience again and again how all measures devised to check disaster prove vain. The breath of death, which might also be a call to awakening, cannot be answered with conscious subtleties; therefore, just as in late classical times, "Dionysus-Hades" becomes again a redeemer.

The Dionysus spirit alone, of course, does not suffice. As we noted earlier, it is extraordinarily important that, in our fresco series, the memory of the Delphic cult be recalled. There Dionysus is not alone; he has been taken up fraternally by the lord of the Delphic temple, Apollo. At Delphi, the dark has found a firm place in the light, and the opposing powers reign there, reciprocally, in a cosmic rhythm that corresponds on a human level with the interchange between waking and dream life. The Delphic Apollo is a symbol for the *consciousness which has accepted what is most foreign to it, the unconscious, as having equal right,* so that a rhythmic correlation arises between the two. We need not say much about this here, for how this working together of consciousness and the unconscious proceeds is symbolized in the fifth scene, in the figure of the *second Silenus*. The way the wine-red cloak of this seated figure wraps its lower half depicts how this Silenus rests firmly in the unconscious. The Dionysian spirit protects and supports him so he can treasure its effects and pass them on to others. But the upper half of his body is entirely light, entirely upright, and his face bears the expression of probing severity. That is an Apollonic appearance: an attentive observation of an event, an order-bringing testing which extends to everything, as the arrows of the far-reaching Apollo reach everywhere. In this sense, the Silenus of the fifth scene is a symbol of calm, conscious, absolute certainty.

Perhaps another small touch from the Delphic mythical associations is of value here. In Delphi, of course, the nine Muses were associated with Apollo and Dionysus as companions and formed a poetic chorus for both gods. This means that a new manner of expression spontaneously arose out of the interaction of consciousness and the unconscious – a new language, so to speak, that no longer obeys only the laws of the rational, but also formulates the irrational so that it can be consciously grasped. In ancient times, *art* was the symbol for this manner of expression which arises from the interchange between waking and sleeping. Art and also philosophy were at that time still creative in a way that we only rarely see today. Both disciplines naturally and authentically include the mythical within themselves. So we see in many Platonic dialogues, for example, that intellectual analysis passes again and again into the mythical realm, and systematic scrutiny alternates over and over with the visionary, so that the impression of a musical antiphony arises for the reader. Plato, indeed, always strives for the beautiful, but his dialogues are often less "beautiful" than astonishing; they are often difficult too because just where they say something important, they go far beyond the esthetic, which is surely a principle of consciousness only. Nevertheless, Plato has been a guide for many later generations for just this reason: the Apollonian and Dionysian appear in his works in a clear, reciprocal arrangement.

In any case, we come to the conclusion that, on the way of individuation for which the fresco series of the Villa of Mysteries is a classic example, a moment comes when consciousness must actively take part in the event. This is the moment of epiphany, which from the point of view of human beings signifies a simultaneous reawakening of the divine. Through this, the Self appears as a spiritual reality, which they must meet with the highest powers of consciousness that have been given to them. The second Silenus in the fifth fresco scene stands as representative for this task. He embodies the plan for all further development. He sets an example which the initiate, in going further, must live up to. How this plan works we shall see in the next fresco scenes.

We might also ask ourselves again whether, in the actual practice of the cult, a superior personality or a "Mana-bearer" placed the plan before the participants in the mystery. Psychologically speaking, this would be possible, although we cannot know for certain. Perhaps the initiates of the private Pompeiian cult were in need of an examiner who, at the right moment, with an inspired "cry of terror" called them back from the idyllic ecstasy of the third scene to their own reality, sending them on their own way. Perhaps they needed a "leader of souls," who gazed after them with attentive sternness when they rushed away, and in so doing thought: "By that which thou doest, will be proved who thou art."

We cannot know these facts. We know only that at all times many women have needed such leaders of souls. I will give only one familiar example. The Catholic Church realized this necessity clearly when, at the time of the so-called Counter-Reformation, it had to win the hearts of people anew. At that time the guidance of souls, especially the souls of women, underwent considerable development by means of priests who sought to understand them as individuals. The greatest Socratic teacher and friend of women at that time was Francois des Sales (1567-1622), a leader of souls, full of Christian love and inexorable severity.[31]

Ideas regarding the psychic necessities of women, which already had been conceived at the time of classical antiquity, expanded in the realm of Christianity and after the time of the Renaissance. They have not been lost since that time either, but have found new forms again in our own time, namely, in the medical guidance of souls as evident in C. G. Jung's work "The Psychology of the Transference."[32] These new forms arise from the inner necessities of modern people. For the more the world is robbed of gods through the advance of natural science, the more the life of the world loses inner meaning. And the more also religious experience splits off, able to manifest itself sometimes only in dreams. For us, dreams are the most eminent "Dionysian" manifestation, and the "Apollonian" examination, which belongs with it, results from the scientific attitude. This is the methodical analysis of dreams.

Before we go further, let us show proof in a brief, modern example of a dream. In it, in somewhat altered form, motifs appear which we have already met. The dream comes from the diaries of the Countess Reventlow, a writer of light genres, who lived from 1871 until 1918. She writes: "23 Sept., 1904. Ridiculous Dreams: About four o'clock in the afternoon I want to go into the primeval forest with a book under my arm and I say to someone: Now is the hour of the apes, now one can dream. I thought at the same time, that in this hour man and ape draw near to one another."[33]

Francisca von Reventlow was an excessively wanton woman who ruined her life in the frenzy at the turn of the last century, when things seemed so gay and were innerly so sad. As the daughter of an old North German family of the nobility, she had to suffer during her youth under the rod of a harsh patriarchy. She should really have become a "Livia," but in protest she became a licentious "Julia." In compensation for this, her dream is not orgiastic, but quiet and entirely sensible. If in the beginning she speaks of "ridiculous dreams," this only shows that she, like countless other people, projects upon her dream life the imbecility of her own waking life. Indeed, one can easily do this as long as one is not scientifically objective toward dreams. Certainly the language of dreams is entirely irrational, and consciousness must, after all, do something to them in order to trace their associations.

The dream starts with a definite time: four o'clock in the afternoon, the time to go into the primeval forest. This "now the time has come" corresponds with the cry of the Dionysian mask of terror; and here, too, it has the effect that the dreamer starts out. Four is the number of psychic wholeness, as Jung conclusively demonstrated in many places, for example, in *Psychology and Alchemy.* Four in the afternoon, when it is about to become evening–that is the time after the *turning point of life* when one must become whole in order to go to meet death.

As the Delphic Thyiades ran into the woods of Parnassus, so the modern dreamer also runs into the woods. But for the countess, no recognizable region is involved; it is the virgin primeval forest into which she goes. She goes into the unknown, the untrodden, since for her there is no mystery cult as there was in ancient times. In her the unknown is untended, wild, and it includes her own neglected shadow side.

The dreamer goes with a book, just as the priestesses in the first scene of the Orphic frescoes carried with them a scroll. This means consciousness must take part in the undertaking, so the dreamer will always know where she is and will not be swallowed by the primeval forest of the unconscious.

The dreamer says: "Now is the hour of the apes; now one can

dream." With this, she expresses clearly the call that has gone out to her. What she calls "ridiculous dreams" are exactly what could make her whole, that is, that which could lead her to becoming a Self. But it is not a god but an *ape* who then draws near this modern woman. This imagery reminds one of the symbolism of the sixteenth modern dream from part two of *Psychology and Alchemy,* in which an ape also appears. Here it is a gibbon who, as this dream says, must be "reconstructed." In the commentary, Jung says that the reconstruction of the ape "can only mean that the anthropoid – man as an archaic fact – is to be put together again."[34] The path therefore clearly "does not lead upwards to the kingdom of the gods and eternal ideas, but down into natural history, into the bestial instinctive foundations of human existence. We are therefore dealing, to put it in classical language, with a *Dionysian mystery.*"[35]

The situation is similar in Reventlow's dream. It might seem astonishing that a woman who was a mere slave to her instincts in such a degrading manner was nevertheless led by the dream not upward but downward, in order to come to herself. What about her licentiousness? It did not by any means signify a true Dionysian life. Francisca von Reventlow was only the prisoner of Titanic greed, which in her time was in conflict with Olympian consciousness. She was one in a mass, one who, together with a thousand others, represented this greed of her time. That she played this role was the curse of this obviously impressionable woman, and she could not escape it by an upward movement but only by a Thyiadic rush into the primeval forest. She had to find the virgin purity of the nature of souls and the unspoiled state of archaic humanity which is not only governed by instinct but also filled with pious obedience. In her dream this is represented by the symbol of the ape. He is the archaic, infantile survivor in herself. In this respect one might describe the ape as a positive shadow side which compensates her negatively colored consciousness.

The ape signifies still more, however, as Jung likewise brings up in his commentary on the dream from *Psychology and Alchemy.* Naturally, I cannot repeat all his thoughts and still extract only what is important for us. He says in part:

This atavistic identification with human and animal ancestors [which corresponds in Reventlow's dream to the rapprochement of man and apes] can be interpreted psychologically as an integration of the unconscious, a veritable bath of renewal in the life-source where one is once again . . . unconscious as in sleep, intoxication and death. Hence the sleep of incubation, the Dionysian orgy, and the ritual death in initiation.[36]

Then Jung speaks of the most significant aspect of the ape symbol. He says that the Greek Hermes Trismegistus, while he stands sponsor to the medieval Mercurius, derives ultimately from the ancient Egyptian Thoth. Jung continues:

The attribute of Thoth was the baboon, or again he was represented outright as an ape. This idea was visibly preserved all through the numberless editions of the Book of the Dead right down to the most recent times. It is true that in the existing alchemical texts – which with few exceptions belong to the Christian era – the ancient connection between Thoth-Hermes and the ape has disappeared [it was offensive because the ape as *simia Dei* was an animal of the devil], but it still existed at the time of the Roman Empire.[37]

The ape is, accordingly, the animal form of Thoth-Hermes, who was the guide of souls through the underworld. As becomes clear from the alchemical Mercurius, the ape embodies the principle and, at the same time, the goal of transformation, that is, of becoming whole.

To make use of these comments for Reventlow's dream, we might perhaps say that this ape appears on the one hand as a symbol for elements of the dreamer's being which have remained archaic and whose integration, with the help of the dream, might lead her to wholeness. On the other hand, the ape is also the *psychopompos* (epithet of Hermes as guide of souls), an archetypal image which draws near to consciousness on the way through the primeval forest of the unconscious in order to guide it. The figure of the Orphic Silenus in our fresco series corresponds to this aspect of the ape. In the third scene, Silenus with his great obesity certainly has a very archaic side also. The demonic, actually the devilish, is then represented in the fifth scene. The Silenus there has above his head the ghostly mask of terror, which promises death and horror as a preliminary to transformation. What Jung adds, in conclusion, in his commentary about the gibbon could also be said about the Orphic Silenus and the ape symbols of the two modern dreamers:

> It is of the essence of the transforming substance to be on the one hand extremely common, even contemptible [like an ape or a drunken Silenus] . . . but on the other hand to mean something of great value, not to say divine. For the transformation leads from the depths to the heights, from the bestially archaic and infantile to the mystical *homo maximus*.[38]

The modern dream parallel shows how, in spite of the differences in the particular symbols conditioned by time, the basic steps of the transformation process are nevertheless completely timeless. Again and again it makes itself felt as an attempt to bring the split-off darkness of the unconscious near the light of consciousness again, bringing about reconciliation of these primeval opposites.

With this, we now turn again to the fresco series of the Villa of Mysteries, where exactly this reconciliation of opposites is represented in the next, the sixth, scene.

The Sixth Scene

In the middle of the back wall of the Initiation Chamber, the *conjunctio* of Dionysus and Ariadne is represented. Unfortunately, the upper part is badly damaged. Only the figure of Dionysus is entirely preserved, so that one sees how he, the redeemer, leans on his beloved, himself redeemed and a picture of peace. Next to him, Ariadne is enthroned and elevated as Persephone. The part of the fresco which portrays the upper half of her body has fallen to ruin. Her lovely right hand, which lies quietly on the shoulder of her beloved, remains and is impressive, as well as the quiet dignity with which she grants him repose at her side.

We have already tried to show briefly in the introduction what this central picture signifies in and of itself. We cannot or dare not speak of this in connection with the fresco series, because we do not know if or in what way something corresponding to this picture might have been brought before the eyes of the participants in the mystery during their initiation. Any kind of conjecture seems useless, all the more because the hint that we can take from the frescoes themselves shows the direction from which we can find a basic connection. It seems highly significant that the human and the legendary figures who have occupied the stage up to now vanish completely at this point. The "forest" has obviously swallowed the initiate who rushed away, and the gate of the inner sanctuary closes against the priestly Silenus and his companions. This disappearance surely points to a *katabasis* – that is, to an entry into the depths of the underworld such as belongs to the dramatic action of many ancient mystery cults. The participants in the mystery then wander through a darkness full of terror in order to find the light of renewal in the depths. For the Orphics, the *katabasis* was the pattern of the path which the initiated had to take again after the death of the body. They learned to know this path during their lives through the symbolic action of the cult, so that after their departure they could surely find it and know for certain that the Lord, who invites all mankind to himself in the same way, will be within reach of their souls.

For the Orphics, the underworld was always the goal of the soul. Their vision found blessedness in those green meadows near the water of life where, in divine twilight, the underground sun of Dionysus was united with the moon of Ariadne. A presentiment of this blessedness opened up to the initiates in the *katabasis* of the mystery cult – indeed just at that moment when they reached the *deepest place* on the way of initiation which was also the turning point from whence a new ascent was possible. That is all we can say here about the moment of *katabasis* in the cult of the Villa of Mysteries, for this is the only point that is confirmed through the representations of the frescoes which follow.

The Seventh Scene

Here we see an indication that the initiate of our cult had to go "through the lower way" in some form during a *katabasis,* for in the first figure of the seventh scene she returns from below, exhausted and wretched. Between the figure of the so-called terrified woman of the fourth scene and the kneeling initiate of the seventh, there exists a clear connection. The terrified woman has made a leap and become a Thyiad; the kneeling woman of the seventh scene is again the Thyiad who comes from below and brings the divine child into the sanctuary of the temple in the form of a phallus lying in the winnowing basket. She is represented as so exhausted, so beside herself, that the allusion to a wild rush to a distant place is certainly not to be overlooked. However, her rush has obviously not led her up to a height, like that of Parnassus, but to a *katabasis,* through the lower way. This – "thou must go through the lower way" – is suited to the degree of consciousness of the Roman woman. Her consciousness was relatively highly developed, and to compensate for this height she needed a corresponding depth. There, however, she found the same mystical light of the divine child as the Delphic women had found on Parnassus.

Before we discuss the seventh scene, it should be mentioned that the motif of *katabasis* is also contained in the story of Orpheus, who was the legendary founder of the Orphic cult. In this well-known story, Orpheus loses his beloved wife Eurydice through death. Hades has torn her away from Orpheus, and so he starts on the road to the underworld to entreat her return from the god of death. His song softens the inexorable harshness of the ruler of shades, who permits Orpheus to lead Eurydice back into the world, but this is only under the condition *that he never look back, but always forward.* This story gives us an indication of what happened to the men after the gate of the temple sanctuary had closed before them. They too must have experienced a *katabasis.* Eurydice is a symbol for the feminine in men, that is, for the soul-image they lose connection with in the course of the development of consciousness. This soul-image falls into the unconscious, and men must climb down into the underworld if they want to win it back and become whole. But in so doing, they dare not glance back. Their eyes must be immutably directed upon the future goal. In the *katabasis,* therefore, the same task is imposed upon men which already faces women at the beginning of the *katabasis;* namely, women must dare to dash into the darkness, but not run back from it. Therefore, neither men nor women can endure the darkening which precedes the transformation unless they are unswervingly mindful of the goal, that is, of rebirth. Both know this goal, for it is given to them as an inheritance from the beginning, in the myth of Dionysus and Ariadne as the divine prototype. Therefore, when they are engaged in the *katabasis,* this prototype – this archetypal image of the *conjunctio* in which we see the reconciliation of the primeval opposites – stands above men and women, pointing the way.

Now at last we turn to the seventh scene and, with this, to the further developments of the initiation way. First of all, I will describe this scene as exactly as possible. It fills the right side of the short, back wall of the Initiation Chamber and stands, therefore, directly to the right of the picture of Dionysus and Ariadne. Since the seventh scene is found on the short wall of the chamber, it, like the fifth scene, surely represents a ceremony in an inner sanctuary. But here we are concerned with a ritual that is reserved for *women alone*. From the seventh scene on, the fresco series includes no masculine figures. The women are now entirely among themselves in the intimacy of a mystery, upon which no alien eye dare fall.

Into this intimacy the initiate returns home with the Dionysian winnowing basket; she is breathless and exhausted, with staring eyes. She has set the basket down before her; she raises herself to her knees and stretches out her arms in order to lift the covering that hides the divine phallus. Her hair is held by a cap; over her left shoulder she still carries the large, heavy torch, which she obviously used just as the Delphic Thyiades did during the nocturnal procession, and which is now extinguished. Many observers of the frescoes have wondered at how badly the figure of this kneeling woman is drawn in comparison with all the other figures in the Initiation Hall. Indeed, she appears remarkably lifeless, with a doll-like stiffness, and the painter seems to have failed with the arms. The only living thing is her overly large eyes, with their suffering glance. One might therefore say she is all eyes. From this point of view, there might be purpose in the unusual representation of this woman. Perhaps it is intended to show us the initiate as entirely caught in a superhuman vision – a vision which her eye can hardly behold. The eyes of human beings are also the expression of their souls. The old philosophical psychology taught that, besides the physical eye, the human being has also an eye of the soul. Just as the physical eye unites human beings with the sun, so the eye of the soul unites them in ecstatic vision with the divine. According to this point of view, the kneeling woman would be an ecstatic visionary; therefore, we might also say she is entirely soul – so much soul that, on this account, she has almost forgotten her body and can no longer move her arms naturally. The image supports such an interpretation.

But before we go further into what this might mean, we will finish describing the seventh scene. Behind the kneeling woman are two more figures of women, unfortunately badly damaged. All that can still be recognized is that the figure further back (next to the kneeling initiate) draws back as though terrified, whereas the closer one moves toward the kneeling initiate and lifts a small, flat basket over her head. Opposite the kneeling woman on the other side of the winnowing basket we then find what is indeed the most impressive figure of the entire fresco series. It is a dark-winged angel, who has dropped down from above in rapid flight. We know this from the way her hair lifts and the folds of her cloak billow out around her knees. Her feet are shod with the Dionysian *cothurni;* they seem now just to touch the ground. But the angel is already in full action. She raises her left hand in a vigorous gesture of repulsion against the kneeling woman; her right hand clasps a long, supple whip, and the right arm, held high, is lifted for a strong blow. (This is what is customarily described as the "flagellation.") The angel's glance goes beyond the seventh scene in the direction she plans to strike. The object of her chastisement is, however, no longer to be seen on the short wall of the chamber. It is the first figure of the eighth scene, with which the next wall begins.

As we see, this scene is mysteriously full of movement and extraordinarily complicated. We will attempt to discuss separately the various figures of the seventh scene, as they appear in turn. With this, we enter into a "primeval forest," so to speak. Because the figure of the angel in this scene has suffered from a noticeably one-sided interpretation – we spoke earlier of the fact that even the Roman Lupercalia were mentioned as parallels – a noticeable falsification has occurred which, I would like to emphasize, Maiuri does not share. He only mentions it, as indeed he cites everything that has been published about the fresco series of the Villa of Mysteries. We are consequently forced to venture an entirely new proposition, and we must be careful to remain entirely unbiased and to view the whole representation purely from a psychological standpoint.

Let us begin, therefore, with the strange, kneeling visionary. This figure is characterized not only by her almost lifeless exhaustion, but also by the *extinguished torch* which she carries. One might consider this torch too as badly drawn. It is clumsy and much too long and heavy in relation to the rather delicate figure of the kneeling woman. It therefore seems a rather unhandy instrument with which to rush through the underworld. The woman must suffer a great deal under this torch, and one asks oneself whether indeed this may be the reason why she appears so weighed down and worn-out. At any rate, this much is certain: the kneeling woman is a torch-swinging Thyiad who has just returned home. But the way she continues to drag the extinguished torch with her and the way it presses on her shoulder indicate something very unusual that cannot be chance, but must be symbolic. While I pondered this problem, it suddenly occurred to me: *the torch is also a stake, and indeed, the woman carries it like a cross.* This is an exciting thought! The stake often replaced the cross in classical antiquity as an instrument of capital punishment, and the older form of crucifixion was impalement. In Gnostic writings, for example, the word "stake" often stands for what we today translate as "cross." In the light of this idea, the torch-stake on the shoulder of the kneeling woman seems to be a symbol of *martyrdom*. The woman bears her cross, but during the *katabasis* this cross has also been both her support and shining light.

This is a symbol one might well be terrified of, for it shows that, for a woman to be a nurse and awakener of Dionysus, she must suffer a veritable martyrdom – something as bad, actually, as the crucifixion of Christ.

As I came to this conclusion, it instantly appeared to me as totally absurd. The comparison of an Orphic initiate with Christ cannot be accepted from any standpoint, for no human woman, not even an Orphic mystagogue, attains in any way, even in the very least, the superhuman figure of Christ. The comparison must therefore be entirely erroneous – or perhaps there is something not quite right with the fresco representation itself. I was prepared therefore to discard at once this train of thought. But then, I could not, for the motif of carrying the cross appears all too cogent to the pictorial representation. We cannot avoid it. We stand, therefore, before a puzzle that cannot be solved.

So let us simply rely on everything that can be objectively stated about the figure of the kneeling initiate. The woman is exhausted; she is beside herself on account of having seen a great vision. Through it, the connection between body and soul has almost broken, and she is now only soul. She carries an extinguished torch which was her shining light in the *katabasis* and has now become an instrument of torture like a cross. This is a symbol that is not readily understandable. We can only note it and proceed from here.

The next question is how the idea of a torch, *which is also a cross,* enters into the Orphic mystery cult. To answer this, we might perhaps take up the symbol of the torch in and of itself. The torch is a primitive lantern, so to speak. It is firewood, for example, that one can kindle at a hearthfire and carry along. Therefore, with the torch we come to the idea of *fire,* and here a further question arises: Where does fire come from in our Orphic cult? From the second to the fifth scene, the Dionysian element has been water. It appeared first of all as holy water; then it appeared in the figure of Silenus, who is a fountain-demon and embodies a divine water; and finally, it appeared in the receptacle of the fifth scene, where it was changed into wine. Already in the wine, the fire creeps into the water, as it were, for wine is a "fire-water."

At this point I discovered a still further connection had escaped me until then, namely, the symbol of the *thyrsus* (staff), which lies over the knees of Dionysus in the central picture of the sixth scene. Let us consider next what was disclosed to us by this important connecting link. The *thyrsus,* which one sees in the hands of the Bacchantes so often in ancient illustrations, was cut from the strong stalk of a bush which in Mediterranean countries can reach up to three meters (ten feet) high. The Greek name of this bush is *narthex;* Latin, *ferula communis;* and German, *steckenkraut* [English, giant fennel – trans.]. The stalk of the *narthex* is hollow, and the Dionysian *thyrsus* was closed at the top with a pine spigot, for it was represented as filled with fire. Here, therefore, we have the idea of fire in the foreground in the central picture of Dionysus. Also, the association of the *narthex* staff with fire is very ancient. According to legend, Prometheus brought the divine fire that he stole from the gods to earth in a *narthex* reed, and since then, the *narthex* is the fire-bearer. With the Dionysian *thyrsus,* the staff is naturally filled with the Dionysian fire. In the central picture of the Dionysian *conjunctio,* the fire consequently becomes a *divine* element. According to our cult then, we see Dionysus, who previously appeared as water and then also as spirit and soul, as divine fire.[39]

The torch of the Thyiad must be sparked by this fire. Just as the Korykian Cave on Parnassus, where Dionysus was resurrected, was at times illuminated by his divine fire to show the way, so the god himself shone in the torches of the Thyiades on their impetuous procession. As we have already seen, the god whose return the illumination marks is, at the same time, himself the illuminator.

The torch is therefore the symbol of divine illumination, which the Thyiadic initiate received during her *katabasis*. And she actually brings this illumination back into the sanctuary; she brings it in entirely objective form, namely, in the form of the winnowing basket with the phallus in it. This is the illumination which the initiate receives: that the god has risen again; that the woman has ecstatically seen, cradled and nourished him; that he has become a creative reality, *palpably near.* But in the meantime, the torch of illumination has been extinguished. It has lasted only an allotted time, as is always the case according to the ancient view. It involves only the brief flare-up of an ecstatic experience, which is once again at an end. If therefore the woman in the temple sanctuary still continues to look toward the divine vision and grasp at it, basically she reaches out into the unreal with unfeeling, dead arms which can grasp nothing. The mystery which she has beheld is now, in daylight, no longer perceptible to her, no longer comprehensible. In wanting to lift the cover which hides the divine phallus from view, she would *commit sacrilege*.

Probably it is in this way that the extinguished torch has now become a cross to the woman. Precisely because it no longer burns, it is an instrument of torture, and therefore the woman is very burdened by it – almost like Christ. But there is still something wrong. The comparison between the initiate and Christ cannot possibly be correct.

You must excuse me if I simply record my thoughts on the representation of the kneeling woman in the seventh scene as they come to me. This scene is so profound and difficult to understand that we can only come to an understanding gropingly and step-by-step.

Therefore, we will again leave the quandary into which we have already stumbled once and turn to the two feminine figures behind the kneeling torch-bearer. With them, fortunately, we stand on somewhat surer ground. In the case of a symbolic series of pictures such as our frescoes, there is a terrible retaliation if one overlooks even one single detail. The pictures one after another present themselves like links in a chain which hangs together; this is also the case with dreams, in which each separate link is important for the entire meaning-connection. I thought at first that the two figures of the women behind the kneeling initiate were too badly damaged to make out anything certain from them. But the basket which the nearer of the two women holds over the head of the kneeling initiate is still preserved, and this symbol gives us a hint about its significance.

The little basket is very flat and, according to Maiuri, contains some twigs of spruce. In classical mystery usage, to hold a basket with the attributes of the mystery god over the head of the participant signifies consecration and benediction after the *katabasis*.[40] The participant in the mystery, who has gone through the mystery death, is returned to life through this benediction and, after an ecstatic experience, is quieted through the god himself.

The *spruce* is one of the most meaningful plant symbols of Dionysus. It was supposed to have been planted at the birth of the god and became then the special symbol for Dionysus-Lysios and of Bacchus, that is, of the god of initiation. According to the old tale, Pentheus was supposed to have climbed a spruce in order to spy on the secret orgies of the Maenads, and the spruce, therefore, was felled by the Maenads. From this spruce the images of Lysios are supposed to have originated; the spruce represents the god himself who protects his mystery from intrusive curiosity. It is also this spruce trunk on which the mask of Dionysus hangs in the temple. As a spruce, Dionysus is especially hidden, the god of the mysteries who himself guards his own secret.

When therefore the little basket with the spruce twigs is held over the head of the kneeling visionary – probably by a priestess of the cult – this is meant to quiet her ecstatic excitement with the blessing of the god and at the same time to remind her to guard herself against intrusive curiosity. So this blessing is at the same time a *warning* to be heeded. That such is intended probably follows also from the gesture of the second woman, still visible behind the kneeling one. What remains in this gesture indicates a terrified retreat. Maiuri too describes it in this way. It is as if she wanted to cry to the kneeling woman, "Go thou not too far."

All this is a most telling confirmation of my impression that something is indeed not right about the kneeling woman of the seventh scene. Her Christ-likeness indicates a dangerous *inflation;* in wanting to raise the cover over the phallus in the winnowing basket, she is, like Pentheus, in danger of climbing the spruce and laying violent hands on the secret of Bacchus. The priestesses behind her wish to quiet her, bless her, and warn her. But the kneeling one pays them no heed. *She has hidden her hair under a cap.* Since hair is a typical symbol for what is in one's head, this probably signifies that she wants to conceal her thoughts and what she has in her head, perhaps also that she shuts herself away from the counsel of others. Blessing and warning cannot reach her.

Indications are that this is an extremely dangerous moment on the initiation path. As the Thyiades could run the wrong way on their nocturnal rush to awakening, according to Delphic legends, so our initiate has also run the wrong way, and the helpful counsel of the priestesses no longer reaches her.

But the initiate is reached by a higher power. The angel swoops down like an eagle with a whirring flap of her wings and raises her hand imperiously against the initiate in a gesture of warding off. This angel is a symbol for which there are parallels from other representations. Maiuri's book about the Villa of Mysteries contains a very nice parallel of this kind.[41] It shows at the left a young satyr; in the middle is a kneeling woman with the winnowing basket who raises her arms to lift the cover from the phallus in it; and at the right is a winged woman's figure with the same gesture of warding off as in our seventh scene. There is another parallel on a mosaic floor from a North African Dionysian sanctuary, where a kneeling woman is portrayed with the winnowing basket (just as in our scene), and near her a nymph floats down with the same gesture of warding off.[42] This representation will interest us again later. Maiuri writes that the figure of the angel which is warding off is held to be a personification of Aidos, that is, the "sense of modesty."

There exists, therefore, the following continuity: during the *katabasis,* in a state of abandon, the kneeling initiate saw the Dionysian creative spirit, and he inspired her to awaken and nourish him. She has brought this vision back to daylight, but she is distraught from its influence and has lost her humanity and feeling. She has become presumptuous and inaccessible to the counsel of others. But here the sense of modesty, which she has lost in face of the holy one, approaches her as a rescuing and avenging angel. This much follows based only upon the fresco representation of the angel without anything further. I know of no parallels in which the angel also raises a whip for a blow.

This is an aspect of the picture which really belongs to the first figure in the eighth scene; we will therefore take up its corresponding symbolism later. There are more things to say about the figure of the angel, and more fundamental ones. Its significance as Aidos-Modesty is only the surface, so to speak. That is, it represents only that part of the angel that refers to the kneeling visionary or, better said, it expresses what the angel says through the language of the picture: "Thou hast no modesty and this is an outrage." This judgment is brought to the kneeling woman through the figure of the angel as an inspiration from on high. The judgment breaks over her as suddenly as the angel breaks into the scene. In doing so, the angel takes command as a feminine messenger of the gods. She wears noticeably high *cothurni,* which shows that she appears in the role of Dionysus. According to this view, the angel is a higher counterpart of the youth in the first scene. As the voice of the god himself spoke from that boy, so here too the god himself speaks out of his winged deputy. This figure stands in the seventh and also in the eighth scene as the *central symbol* uniting both scenes. This time, however, it is not a human being, but a winged spirit of the air through which the god speaks to the initiate. He who earlier ruled through fire and "fired" the initiate appears now as a *spiritus aerëus* or *volans* and, through this, the *air now becomes a Dionysian element.*[43]

As divine breath, the air, which appears embodied in the angel, has the character of a *pneuma.* Just as earlier, in the symbol of the wine, the divine fire was symbolized as hidden in the water, so the fire in the pneuma is thought of as hidden in the air. The pneuma is a fiery air or a fiery wind. So that we may better grasp the significance of the figure of the dark-winged angel in the seventh scene, I must go more closely into the ancient idea of the pneuma. In this, I refer to Leisegang, who says expressly – in the last chapter of *Der Heilige Geist* – that the cult of Dionysus is the cradle of all ancient teachings about the Holy Ghost which are found anywhere in Greek literature. From this we can gather that it is not unlikely to conceive of the angel figure of our frescoes as a pneuma.

According to old linguistic usage, the pneuma is simply moving air or breath: the breath of the wind, the breath of human beings, the gods, and also of animals – that is, generally, the breath of life. According to the popular view, souls hover in the dark air under the moon, and demons also are *pneumata.* Moving air is the carrier of all spirits and all powers of life; the winds are also fertility demons. These old concepts were elaborated upon in the Orphic cult. This cult saw the air peopled with souls; winds carried souls into human beings, and after death the human breath spirit flowed together with the divine pneuma. In the understanding of the Stoics, pneuma, as air, is a constituent element in the Cosmos; besides, it is *unalloyed inner knowledge*. As such, it is not thought of as ideas, but as divine power, which is operative in mankind as well as in the Cosmos. Therefore it is within and without, in a similar fashion. Poseidonius says: "The First Principle is matter and spirit, and as such a delicate, fiery pneuma. This is eternal and immortal."[44]

The pneuma is a body, the finest of all, that which permeates everything. It holds dead masses together and is the life-force of animal being, the carrier of souls and spiritual activity in human beings. Finally, it is the intelligence of the world. Through the pneuma, the spirit penetrates everywhere. This is a concept which the Stoics also formulated through the idea of the *logoi spermatikoi,* those spiritual germs which constantly rain out of ether onto the earth, which are at the same time airy and fiery. In this sense, the Holy Ghost of antiquity – that which reaches all, permeates all – is also that which *unites* all. It governs in all so that, as the Stoics said, no event stands alone.[45] Therefore omens exist, which can be interpreted because of the pneumatic connection of all events.

About this great theme I can naturally make only suggestions. But at least something may still be added: as unalloyed inner knowledge, as the divine power in humanity, the pneuma has also a *moral* significance, namely, that of self-knowledge. The pneuma is the truly human in humanity, procreator, accuser, and ruler; it is the agent which guides human beings. In this regard, Poseidonius compared it also with the daimon of Socrates. As the truly human, the pneuma emerges suddenly in the mortal. As Philo of Alexandria formulates it: "It rises unforeseen and unhoped for, as the 'startling light of self-taught wisdom'."[46] Leisegang says it would be most correct to say the pneuma expresses the soul of the human being, since that is its active part.

One thing remains to be said. According to the conceptions in the old Dionysian religion and also in Orphic tradition, the god is a being similar to a human being. Dionysus is everything – god, man, and nature; and in *enthusiasm,* the state of being filled with god, unity with the Dionysus-Allbeing is experienced. Dionysian enthusiasm, which is exactly the experience of the pneuma, is a *theia mania,* a divine madness. For the Greeks, madness was originally a divine punishment, as we know, for example, from the Orestes story; but in the cult of Dionysus, the curse becomes a mystical gift of grace, like the miracle of Pentecost.

In the angel figure of the seventh scene, the Holy Ghost of the Orphic cult darts down with a dark beating of wings, which signifies a deeply moving turning point in the dramatic action. For we have just seen the phallus in the winnowing basket as the symbol of the god. It is a symbol that, if it does *not* remain hidden, has a grotesque and obscene character. In Greek comedy, which indeed grew out of the cult of Dionysus, a more than lifesized phallus appeared as a requirement in the scenes of grossness. In the festival processions of the peasants, it was carried across the stage as an attribute of the god, and the peasants themselves appear as *ithyphallic* (erect phallus). The phallus in the winnowing basket is therefore an extremely ambiguous symbol: it is *also* indecent. But in Greece the indecent belonged precisely to women's mysteries as an important constituent. In the Eleusinian Mysteries, for example, women came together to exchange indecent jokes, and this was a religious rite. And as embodiment of the indecent, there appears in the Eleusinian myth the earthly Baubo, who cheers up the sorrowing Demeter by an improper gesture.[47]

For this reason, the seventh scene of the fresco series surely took place among women alone in the privacy of the Holy of Holies. In the symbolism of the winnowing basket, the indecent plays a part. The phallus remains covered, to be sure; nevertheless, it becomes clear that sex awakens when the divine child is awakened. The illumination which the initiate brings back into the temple from the *katabasis* is not at all what one might call a high point. On the contrary, it is a deep-as-the-underworld, Dionysian secret that the divine spirit manifests itself to women in sex. This secret must remain strictly hidden, for uncovered it would become the cheapest thing there is.

It is this implication of cheapness which has led certain scholars to think of the Roman Lupercalian feasts as parallels. These were puberty celebrations at which the actual, physical generative power of youths and the bodily fertility of women took first consideration.

But this is exactly what is *not* meant here. In antiquity, the old idea was everywhere alive that the *unio mystica* of the human with the divine was also a sexual union. This was often represented in the mystery plays – in Greece, for example in Athens, as well as in Eleusis. And we know that the mysteries of Isis in Rome were repeatedly indecent for just this reason, because in them a *unio mystica* was dramatically represented.[48]

It is a truly divine recognition that sex too can be holy. And for a woman it is truly one of the most important experiences that the creative spirit becomes alive for her when it reaches her bodily depths. As Poseidonius said, the Original Principle is matter and spirit. For human beings the two are united in sex – the Original Principle within themselves. But this is an *arrhēton,* an ineffable secret. The initiate of our cult experienced it in the divine madness of an enthusiasm. She has cast herself toward death, and in an illumination she has experienced the deep and simple mystery of spiritual life.

Concerning the symbolism of the seventh scene, we can quote the often cited sentence of the alchemical *Tabula Smaragdina:* "What is below is as that which is above; and what is above is as that which is below; in order that the miracles of the *one* thing may be accomplished."

In our Orphic cult the "one thing" is Dionysus as the Self and at the same time also as becoming a self. For a woman, this appears above all as a coming into being of the spirit. Through the Dionysian phallus, the initiate experienced the spirit as male generative power. This is the thing below, and through this she becomes inflated, so that she feels like a bearer of the cross. Because of the experience of the divine generative power, she has fallen into *theia mania*. She is nothing more than this madness – a holy, raving seeress – and she considers this complete fulfillment. But already the thing below changes into the thing above, and the masculine changes into the feminine. The spirit of Dionysus swoops down upon the initiate as feminine pneuma – a dark angel – in order to bear witness to her true humanity. As feminine pneuma we might describe the angel also as Sophia; this is surely the "startling light of self-learned wisdom" of which Philo speaks, that *strikes* the initiate unawares, accusing, ruling and mediating. What the angel mediates, above all, is the *spiritual feeling of modesty* as a gift of grace of the Holy Ghost. Through this symbolism, perhaps we modern women may also receive illumination. Or do we all know that, for a woman, the feeling of modesty is the first and highest requisite, precisely in relation to the experience of the spirit?

At the same time, the pneuma-Sophia figure mediates to the initiate yet another startling illumination. The angel, as manifest bearer of the Dionysian *theia mania,* stands face to face with the initiate. The angel shows her that it is not *she* who has the gift of the seer. The Holy Ghost has filled her for a brief moment, and already, with a powerful warding-off movement of the hand, the angel cuts off from itself again the mortal being who is certainly not "Christlike." Through this appearance – an act of grace – the angel *differentiates* the woman from the higher femininity of Sophia, who she herself never is.

The seventh scene, therefore, shows the picture of an illumination and a profanation that cannot be warded off through human help, but can be set right only through the intervention of a higher power. It portrays with dramatic impressiveness a moment of the utmost danger on the mystery way. Only one movement too many, and the divine secret becomes lost forever and life becomes a "drama of grossness."

Only an act of grace can prevent this terrible loss. That there is such a moment on the way of psychic transformation has been perceived by human beings in all times and has been expressed symbolically. In Iranian mythology, for example, its symbol is the dangerous bridge Cinvat, which leads over an abyss. For the good (who is good?) the bridge is wide. For all others narrow as a knife-edge.[49]

This is a symbol that appears also in modern dreams in manifold variations. It signifies that at this moment everything stands on knife's edge, in that the slightest false movement would cast the human being into an abyss. The idea of a deadly peril being connected with the path of inner development could almost make one despair. But certainly human life is always threatened with perils. As the wisdom of all peoples teaches, every living person is always "encompassed by death." Only *spiritual death* is in a certain sense without danger; this death ensues when a person does not follow the call of the "mask of terror," which heralds introversion and transformation. If the transformation is refused, inner development comes to a standstill and the person's psyche dries up. Such a dried-up person has no more problems, no tasks lie before him, and it does not matter what becomes of the living corpse. Then all danger of death and all terror are saddled on the outer world. That is, everything deadly and all dark devilry are projected into the world, and then everything frightful stands on knife's edge in the world. That is why the initiations and mystery cults of all peoples and all times teach the individual who is ready and able for advancement to go to face his own danger. For it is in accordance with universal human experience that, for the individual just then, when everything in him stands on knife's edge and danger is greatest, the most powerful help might draw near him like the beating of a dark angel's wings.

For all ancient mystery cults, as Karl Kerényi said, this saying is valid: *ho telos ho gamos* (the goal of initiation is union). In the puberty consecrations of boys and girls, the goal is physical copulation, which previously signified an ineffable mystery for the children. The capacity to mate and to hand life on from generation to generation is bestowed on the boys and girls in the first consecration as a divine gift. Generative power penetrates them as natural desire, and therefore the Roman Lupercalian festivals, which brought to a close the puberty initiations of boys, were always a popular diversion. But in the higher initiation of the grown person, the goal is the mysterious union of the human soul with the spirit of God – a sacred marriage that is supposed to make people "twice-born" and bring them immortality. Again sex is animated; again desire stirs. Goethe expressed it beautifully and tenderly in his poem "Selige Sehnsucht" (Blessed Longing):

Nicht mehr bleibest du umfangen
In der Finsternis Umschattung
Und dich reisset neu Verlangen
Auf zu höherer Begattung. . . .

No longer remainest thou encompassed
In the shades of darkness
And new desire inflames thee
To a higher union. . . .

In such a way the initiate of the seventh scene is represented: she is drawn upward, torn out of consciousness through Dionysian enthusiasm into an experience that greatly exceeds all human consciousness and therefore is rightly experienced as an exaltation. Nevertheless, the place of this higher experience always remains the same. *Ho telos ho gamos;* the goal is always union. The mystery experience decisively touches upon sex as an experience of depth, where the divine and the animal, the holy and the indecent are indissolubly united. Therefore a strange ambiguity creeps into the symbolism of the seventh scene, as we saw was also included in the holy, healing figure of Baubo; and it stands on a knife's edge whether or not the highest will reverse itself into the cheapest. Therefore, the angel figure of the seventh scene bears also the traditional features of Aidos: she embodies, for the initiate, the feeling of modesty as the light of wisdom.

We must now try to come somewhat nearer to these associations from a psychological standpoint. I can, of course, give only a few more or less scattered suggestions here, for it is a very ticklish field. To achieve a certain understanding, let us first cast a backward glance to the spiritual development of the initiate up to this point on the way of initiation. In this connection I would like to bring to our aid certain ancient views about human nature, known through Gnosticism, but which, as Leisegang believes, go back to much older times.[50] According to this classical view, human beings have three natures: namely, the *hylic,* the *psychic* and the *pneumatic.* Accordingly one can speak also of hylic, psychic and pneumatic people.

Hylic people are material and carnal, identified with their bodies; in other words, they are natural human beings with their primitive, instinctual basis. The way of initiation in our Orphic cult is concerned first with this kind of human being who is in thrall to nature. The initiate, as a carnal human being, is first released from entanglement with the Titanic greed of her time; and in the second scene, through a sacrament, she is again grounded in the purity of her primitive instincts. Along with this, as symbol of her awakening psychic nature, there also appears the twig of laurel that symbolizes a germ or a promise of spiritual growth. In the laurel twig we see the spiritual possibilities of development of the initiate as they belong inherently to natural or hylic human beings. If they are genuine and true, here is the first nature-given totality from which they can function instinctively, free and whole, in connection with cosmic order. This ability is represented in the third scene, where the initiate appears as a kid. Here again she is reinstated into the wholeness of the natural scheme of things, where Dionysus rules as the hidden light of nature, lending meaning to whatever befalls. The kid is the symbol of the genuine hylic human being, whose reinstatement was a prerequisite to the Orphics for further initiation. And with this, the special spirituality of the woman reveals itself in a new form, that is, as the observant young buck that stands in the foreground of the third scene. The same spirituality that had previously sprouted in the laurel twig (concealed still and split-off, so to speak) appears now as a warm-blooded creature, akin to the femininity of the initiate – as the young buck who belongs to the kid and, with it, makes a pair.

If in order to understand better, one dares draw upon modern terminology, one can describe this young buck as a first form of the animus, a still subhuman form, to be sure, but suitable to the initiate on this initial level, for certainly she is not yet reborn into true humanity. She is still a hylic person; this condition is pure, and she is ready to receive the mystery of the psyche. This readiness, a given spiritual attitude at this level, is represented by the little buck, who harkens so attentively to what the future may hold. It is this that the animus can mediate to the woman from the beginning – indeed, even in animal form – namely, the right spiritual attitude necessary to a given situation. Here, as I have said, this right attitude is an attentive readiness, one which brings it about that, while the initiate cannot see the god as spirit, yet she can hear him. It is actually represented this way in the so-called terrified woman of the fourth scene. With the help of the little buck, she has been able to hear the call of the mimes of terror, and she starts on the path of the *katabasis*.

When in the seventh scene, we see the initiate return from the *katabasis* which she has accomplished, we recognize that she has been transformed. In the *katabasis* she has found her psychic nature, and now, with her too-large seer's eyes, she is seen as entirely soul. But during this process she has again forgotten the hylic or natural aspect, which she certainly also has. In the divine drama which she has experienced, her connection with her natural reality and with her body has been lost, and it is this, properly speaking, that is her guilt and her presumption.

We have seen in the discussion of the third scene that the reinstatement of naturalness is the decisive step in the Orphic cult. It was precisely through this that Orphic initiates could legitimize themselves even beyond death – that they dare say, "I became a god, for I became both kid and buck." One of the fundamental recognitions of Orphic teachings is that the entirely natural is also the divine in human beings, if it is truly pure. The instinctual nature of human beings was accepted by the Orphic cult, in this particular sense. This possibility of recognizing divinity in nature was bestowed upon the Orphic by the ruling figure of Dionysus; for Dionysus, besides being god and human, is certainly nature also. To neglect or forget the physical person and his natural impulses is a serious guilt which must avenge itself. This is true everywhere and at all times: no person is ever entirely soul. Wherever we go we must indeed take the little kid and the little buck with us; we must let the divine gift of the pure instinctual basis always take a part in ruling and speaking. Otherwise, we are terribly incomplete. It is very meaningful that the kneeling initiate of the seventh scene is represented as so stiff and doll-like, unalive and even ugly. It represents her incompleteness; she has become one-sided – now only soul. Or perhaps one should say she is now only a ghost.

Judging by the representation in the seventh scene, the animus of the initiate has also accomplished a transformation. Through the figure of the little buck, he appeared as youthful, passionate, even demonic impulse. In the *katabasis,* however, he has again taken on vegetable form; he appears now as the torch which lights the path of the initiate in the underworld. This is wood, and so it is a counterpart of the little twig of laurel in the second scene which embodies imperceptible, spontaneous, spiritual growth. But this growth has now achieved maturity; the sprig in the second scene has grown up to a certain extent in the seventh, becoming a bearer of light. The burning torch shows the animus of the woman in his real function *as guide and mediator* between her consciousness and the contents of the collective unconscious. And in a similar way, the anima can appear to the man as a bearer of light; this is, indeed, a common symbol. (A lovely example is contained in the dream of Poliphilo.)

The soul-image in its archetypal role as mediator is essentially a bearer of light. The light of the unconscious reaches consciousness in this symbol, and in this sense the torch is a spark from the divine light of the Self, which is what Dionysus stands for in the Orphic cult. While consciousness is obscured in the *katabasis* so that only the dreaming eye of the imagination seems to live, the torchlight of the soul-image illuminates the goal of life in the symbol of the sacred union of Dionysus-sun and Ariadne-moon. Through this drama, the goal for the woman all at once becomes so alive that it is as though it were a new-born divine child. At the same time, she realizes that, here in the unifying symbol of the Self, the eternal generative power is contained from which all life of the soul arises. Through this too, the soul of the woman comes alive, as though she were newly raised from the dead. The drama, which is at the same time the knowledge of good and evil (a Gnosis), is what can make the hylic person whole – as the ancients said, into a twice-born human being. It is mediated to the woman's consciousness by the divine-demonic symbol of the animus, which resembles the spiritual aspect of the Self, or mirrors it. The torch, as seen from its shape, is also a phallic symbol for "the creative" in the soul of the woman that can bring itself to life and impregnate her so that she becomes a form of the spirit. The visionary drama is such a form; that is why, in the seventh scene, it is represented as an actual *form,* namely, as the winnowing basket with the phallus in it. However, in order that this drama may become actuality and may be held fast in reality, the initiate dare not lose sight of her own naturalness. The place where the psychic can realize itself permanently is – to speak in the language of antiquity – always the hylic, that is, one's own body and one's own entirely ordinary reality. Without that, the person has no roots in himself, and what is he then?

With this, we come to the symbol of the initiate as cross-bearer. She is represented dragging the extinguished torch as though she had attached to it. She cannot put it away, in spite of the fact that in the temple sanctuary she can certainly no longer use it. Psychologically, this symbolism signifies the attempt of the woman to hold fast and perpetuate in a certain form the constantly varying and changing image of the soul; but this means nothing other than that the woman *identifies* with it. The woman who is only soul or only spirit – this is indeed the *animus-possessed* woman. She thinks she now has the spark of the spirit which guides her, but the animus is an autonomous factor of the collective unconscious, which one cannot possess. At most one is stifled by it, as by an instrument of torture.

It is due to the negative aspect of the *theia mania* – that is, the divine seizure of the religion of Dionysus – that this is also a phenomenon of primitive, demonic possession. To heal and quiet this, a corresponding primitive *rite de sortie* is necessary, which takes human beings out of possession and returns them to ordinary humanity. Such a *rite de sortie* is represented in the seventh scene of our fresco series in the ritual performance of the two priestesses with the little basket. This little basket filled with spruce boughs is held over the head of the initiate so she may realize how far the divine – in this case, Dionysus as spruce – stands above her and that she should not lay violent hands upon it.

But the blessing and warning gesture of the priestesses is to no avail, because under her cap the initiate has her own thoughts in her head, from which all exhortation glances off. It is not hard to imagine what kind of hidden thoughts those are. Just because the initiate is portrayed as an enthusiastic seeress, she obviously thinks she has already reached the highest level of the initiation; she has become a *pneumatic* person who, as the ancients said, needs no more earthly food, because seeing has become her food – one whose spirit reaches above itself out into the sphere of the divine. It is the secret illusion of the initiate that she has become the feminine counterpart of the ecstatic Silenus of the third scene, which in our fresco series symbolizes the pneumatic man, the highest half-divine level of all human existence. In other words, the initiate deceives herself that she has become a very great "medicine woman," a Mana-personality like Silenus. This is, of course, reflected in the remarkable "Christ-likeness" of her picture, which is, at the same time, her martyrdom.

In this regard we see the dangerous, deceptive effect that the archetypal image of the animus can have. As soon as the woman identifies with it, she is helplessly in the power of his dark, demonic effect. The extinguished torch is the symbol of this. It shows the extinguishing, mist-bringing effect of the image of the soul on which the woman has laid violent hands. If the woman claims the divine laurel for herself, it becomes a dead and deadly piece of wood on which she is almost destroyed.

If we look for a parallel to the symbol of the extinguished torch, we find in later times a very striking and widely known one, namely, the dead wood of the witch's broom upon which the witch travels to the Blocksberg. Here too the woman is perceived as demonic and unwholesome because she thinks she possesses a demonic spirit; nevertheless, it is she who is possessed. In this connection it is interesting to think that the witch of the Middle Ages was generally depicted as shameless. And indeed, this never referred primarily to outer, ordinary disorderly behavior. The common report about witches was always that they carried on lewdly with demons. There are highly learned writings of the Middle Ages in which this is very drastically represented.[51] At the witches' trials, prosecutors always tried to show evidence of witches' lewdness with demons. Here the primitive idea of the *spiritus familiaris* played a special role. The *spiritus familiaris* of the witch was usually a small animal (for example, a toad), and it was claimed that the witch hid it with her in the house and suckled it like a nurse. The frog, which is very like a human being, is really a symbol for the small child, and because of this the witch who nurses it stands in the role of a Delphic Thyiad, who became nurse to the divine child. But because in the Christian era everything Dionysian was rejected and accursed, the divine child in the Middle Ages – a symbol of the light of the unconscious – became nothing but an evil, ghostly toad, and the woman in whom this light arose as a spark of the spirit, nothing but a criminal. The old pagan background lived on in the Christians of the Middle Ages as a sinister, evil witches' kitchen in which the split-off shadow figure of Dionysus ruled as a gigantic, obscene, satanic buck. Here nothing stood on knife's edge; the fateful grasp which uncovered the divine mystery of the phallus happened irreparably in the witchcraft of the Middle Ages; the humble, pious Baubo, who bore the good tidings of the "higher copulation" to the sorrowing Demeter, became then nothing more than a demonic, lascivious old woman.

The witches of the Middle Ages could not help remaining bound to the deadly, mist-bringing wood of the witches' broom; the Dionysian side of the feminine spirit could certainly not develop in the Middle Ages; it was damned by the church. This was a necessary condition of the times. The church of the Middle Ages had to guard the individual from regressing into paganism's thralldom to nature. But on this account, women especially fell under a terrible yoke: the dark, Dionysian side of the anima, which was also damned, was of course projected on them so that many women were bound by men with the men's own unholy and demonic fantasies. None of this could be changed for either men or women until nature as a whole was released from both devilish and divine attributes to be seen as it really is. This task has been accomplished by scientists, and as a result the human being too seems to have been released from devilish attributes as well as from divine ones and to have been reinstated in his hylic nature.

So now, apparently, the problem posed by the seventh scene of our fresco series, as well as the problem of the nature of witches, no longer concerns us today. Modern psychology has again discovered the psychic nature of man, and C. G. Jung has pushed forward into those depths in all modern persons where the Dionysian-Mercurian spirit – as the spiritual nature of the unconscious – is still always alive and active, and ever renewed. He has discovered that it can be highly dangerous not to concern ourselves with this, and that for modern women a spiritual development is also available similar to that which the initiation way of the Pompeiian fresco series symbolically shows. Within modern women too grows a twig of laurel; modern women too have spiritual impulses within them, which look very much like an aggressive young buck; modern women too can be driven out of their natural relatedness and out of the things they are bound up in by the terrifying spiritual call of the turning point of life; and then they too are plunged into the suffering and the darkness of a *katabasis*. If then, a woman does nothing about this, she becomes dead wood, befogged and befogging her surroundings. Therefore it is necessary for a woman to learn to take note of and hold fast to what the torchlight of the image of the soul brings her from the depths of the unconscious.

What the people of old represented dramatically in a ritual *katabasis* is in our modern form a private, methodical activity, namely, a dialogue with the torch-bearer and a recording of what he shows us. The technical term for this is "active imagination." One might think this to be the most harmless activity there is. But it is not, if only because the torch of the animus always illuminates also the being of the woman. He is a mirror for the most painful self-recognition; he appears always clothed in our own shadow side, and if he shows himself power-mad or malicious, for example, he is so because we are so. Aside from this, in the imaginative drama which the guiding animus mediates to her, the woman is confronted with the contents of the collective unconscious and as a result is also exposed to its overpowering effects. In order to resist these effects, we can indeed note certain practical ways and means for ourselves which we learn from experience. But human wits are very small over against the things which consciousness never has the capacity to grasp. Therefore in this stage of her development, the modern woman too falls into the danger of being pulled upward and out of herself, just like the woman of antiquity, so that, in the power of the experience, she forgets her ordinary humanity and thinks she is entirely soul or entirely spirit. For her too, the image of the guide can become an extinguished, befogging torch, which weighs upon her and torments her, at the same time making a fool of her by creating the illusion of god-likeness.

Through her identification with the image of the animus, which is symbolized in the seventh scene by the carrying of the extinguished torch, the natural flow of psychic life is sorely disturbed for the woman. As we said before, such an identification signifies an attempt to perpetuate a definite outward shape for the highly variable animus-image. Then psychic energies can no longer flow on toward new development; they become dammed up and begin to stream back into the unconscious. This constitutes a regression through which, below the threshold of consciousness, the repressed thralldom to nature gains an excessive and negative power. The old impulse, which is symbolized in our fresco series as the *little buck,* receives a too great influx of energy, so that he grows threateningly and becomes heated. However, where the little buck stands, there is always the little kid nearby; and through the regression, it too becomes disturbing and negative.

In the development of many modern women, there is a phase where one can clearly observe the destructive influence of the "little buck" and "little kid," brought about by such a regression. On the one hand, through the little buck, which represents the subhuman aspect of the animus, the spiritual activities of women who are in themselves highly developed can appear contaminated by a smouldering, underground fire. They became feverish and have something exhausted about them. But on the other hand, the natural Eros, which is symbolized by the little kid of our frescoes, obtrudes itself into their spiritual life in an unnatural and compulsive way. The eroticism of such women takes the *wrong direction,* as it were – namely, over and *above nature,* so that they stretch out lifeless, insensible arms toward the concealed mystery of the creative spirit, thereby committing sacrilege. An animus-possessed woman is also always delivered over to her split-off Eros or – better said – she is torn hither and yon between the spirit which rules her and a compulsive, unconscious eroticism. In the Middle Ages, this phenomenon expressed itself in the fantasy of the lewdness of witches with demons.

We must mention these things, for even if we no longer share the concreteness and negativity of the Middle Ages toward the manifestations of the unconscious, they nevertheless belong essentially to the problem of women. They are also important for men to know about because, through the anima, men share in a corresponding problem. Just as women can become animus-possessed, so men can become anima-possessed, and then for them too the doors to the witches' kitchen open. Indeed, it is described this way in the first part of Goethe's *Faust,* for example; in the tragedy of Gretchen this drama describes the evil that can come of it.

Scientifically expressed, animal- or anima-possession, as we have already said, signifies an identification with the soul-image, and since this has an archetypal character, it signifies at the same time an *inflation.* This is the frightful danger for modern persons too, when during the individuation process everything stands on knife's edge. If their egos are identified with the soul-image, consciousness becomes defenselessly blinded by the celestial-infernal light of the Self, and then one cannot know what may happen to them. C. G. Jung emphatically confirmed this, for example, in his important essay "Concerning the Self":

> I should like to mention only that the more numerous and the more significant the unconscious contents which are assimilated to the ego, the closer the approximation of the ego to the Self, even though this approximation must be a never-ending process. A repression and at the same time an inflation of the ego ["Mana-personality"] results unavoidably. . . . Anyone who has to deal with such cases knows how dangerous an inflation can be. No more than a flight of steps or a smooth floor is needed to give the individual a fatal fall. Besides the "casus ab alto," there are other factors of a no less disagreeable psycho-somatic and psychic nature which serve to reduce "puffed-up-ness." This condition must not be interpreted as one of conscious self-aggrandizement. Such is far from being the rule. In general, we are not directly conscious of the condition, but at best we can deduce its existence indirectly from symptoms. These include the reactions of our immediate environment. For inflation augments the blind spot in the eye; and the more we integrate of the projection-forming factor, the greater becomes our inclination to identify with it. A clear symptom pointing to this fact is the isolation from our surroundings that sets in at such a moment and our attendant disinclination to note or heed the reactions found there.
>
> It must be accounted a psychic catastrophe when the *ego is assimilated by the Self.* The Self remains in the unconscious except for those greater or

smaller portions which are admitted to consciousness. Therefore, on the one hand, it shares the archaic nature of the unconscious; on the other, it has the character of moving within a space-time continuum that is entirely relative to the psyche. Both these properties are numinous and hence have an unlimited determining influence upon the ego-consciousness, which is differentiated, that is, separated, from the unconscious, and yet at the same time exists in an absolute space and an absolute time. That this should be so is a vital necessity. If therefore the ego comes for a certain length of time under the control of one or another unconscious factor, its adaptation is disturbed and the way is opened for all sorts of possible accidents.

Hence the importance must not be underestimated of anchoring the ego in the world of consciousness by a very precise *adaptation*. For this, certain virtues like attention, conscientiousness, patience, etc., are of great value on the moral side; just as a careful consideration of the symptomatology of the unconscious and an objective self-criticism are valuable on the intellectual side.[52]

This very concentrated discussion is not entirely easy to understand, but it expresses accurately, in the scientific language of modern psychology, what we have seen in the symbolic-mythological language of our fresco series. The representation of the ancient way of initiation shows us how it looks when contents of the unconscious are assimilated into the ego. In the seventh scene then, the initiate is represented as having actually approached the Self, in that she kneels directly before the divine symbol of the winnowing basket; and her inflation is mirrored by the fact that she stands there at the same time as an enthusiastic seeress or – in the ancient terminology – as a pneumatic being. She experiences herself as a Mana-personality like the ecstatic Silenus of the third scene.

Jung's express declaration that no conscious arrogance is to be understood in this condition of inflation is important in this regard. This is as little the case in the representation of the seventh scene as it is with certain modern women who become puffed up in the course of the individuation process from the imaginative play which the animus mediates to them. As Jung says, one simply cannot become directly conscious of an inflation. Because she cannot attend to the priestessess who wish to help her, the initiate of the seventh scene slides to her knees, so to speak – in a condition of exhaustion – into the inflation of being the bearer of the cross. She is unable to receive the counsel of the priestessess simply, in good faith.

This is the case for modern people in still greater measure. We too can no longer simply *believe*. The capacity for the blind, child-like belief is lost to most of us. We must let ourselves be led up to the danger line of inflation, like the initiate of the Pompeiian cult, who obviously represents a creature of late antiquity who also could not simply believe. For we must *experience* for ourselves that there are psychic factors in which, along with the power and the deadly danger, there also lies the only source of the help we need for becoming whole. For very many modern people, only this experience is convincing. The terrible danger of inflation which emerges at this moment can only be inferred from the presence of corresponding symptoms, as Jung states. Symptoms of this sort are represented in the seventh scene of our frescoes by the stiff lifelessness of the initiate, a phenomenon that can also show itself clearly in modern women; for example, it may take the form of unspeakable boredom or of enthusiastic or, indeed, melodramatic excitement which can cause the body to suffer most severely. Many modern women, to be sure, can hide such symptoms very skillfully under a cap, just like our initiate, especially when they succeed, in addition, in making soulful eyes. But the human environment reacts to such attempts at concealment much more acutely than one thinks in the unsuspectingness of one's puffed-up-ness; it rejects the expressions of inflation with fear and with attempts at quieting, like the two priestesses who stand behind our initiate with their significant little basket. Many modern women, then, are very like the initiate of the seventh scene: under these circumstances they may already be so carried away from all natural human contact by the inflation, and so isolated, that they can no longer take notice of the friendly counsel of bystanders.

What is needed then, perhaps, is a flash of lightning out of the clear sky descending like the winged Dionysian pneuma of the seventh scene, to set the person straight and, through a shock, to impart insight into the moral necessity of "certain virtues" – as Jung says–which in an inflation are the redeeming thing. It is extraordinarily significant that, along with the severe disturbance and confusion which it depicts, the seventh scene of the Pompeiian frescoes also sets the *moral problem* so clearly in the foreground, in the figure of the dark-winged angel.

In this sense the ancient way of initiation is a close parallel to the way of individuation for modern people, who through it are also always presented with fundamental moral problems. But this process is never concerned with a morality which we already know, never with principles of our ethical consciousness, but with a higher, and at the same time deeper, morality which, like every redeeming thing, springs from the original ground of the soul itself. And so no matter how it is brought to us–as a bolt of lightning or as the unexpected, dark beating of wings of a Sophia–we must accept it.

According to the representation of the seventh scene, the virtue which is necessary for the woman especially (as against the danger of inflation), that which breaks in upon her like a startling new enlightenment, is the *feeling of modesty.* It is certainly an entirely unexpected development that the dark angel of this fresco should at the same time embody a sense of modesty; but this is typical, for the virtues we need for inner development can only be unexpected. They are just those virtues which we do *not* possess consciously.

We must reflect upon this somewhat more in detail. Christian culture, unlike most other cultures, has placed the sense of modesty in the foreground, especially in relation to women. For Christendom, womanly modesty is actually their fundamental virtue. Above all, this relates to bodily and sexual life, and in the course of modern times–especially in the nineteenth century, as Christianity became more and more identified with morality–it has been stressed to an extreme extent. In the nineteenth century, people–and especially women–existed only down to their waist, so to speak, and everything below became an *arrheton,* an ineffable, holy-unholy secret. Today we have still not overcome this viewpoint, and indeed not even those women who fall to the other extreme out of protest against past moral precepts, who often produce in dress and behavior every other effect than that of modesty. Most of us are still far from that pure naturalness in relation to the life of the body and sexuality which the Orphic mystery cult symbolizes with the reinstatement of the little kid. We are either too pure – which can express itself perhaps in the craze for cleanliness or as frigidity – or too impure, which often shows itself in the actually challenging "war paint" of many who in themselves are entirely upright women.

But the symbolism of the seventh fresco scene does not concern itself at all with these problems. The dark figure of the angel appears to the initiate as a personification of the sense of modesty at the moment when she has achieved an extreme point in her spiritual development, when she has become identified with the animus and is on the point of committing sacrilege against the spirit. The scene must, therefore, be concerned with a sense of modesty related to the manifestations of the spirit. That such a sense of modesty could and must exist for them, most modern women little realize – as little as the Orphic initiate represented in the Pompeiian frescoes. Modern women too, just in the decisive phase of their psychic-spiritual development, can be driven by an unconscious, compulsive eroticism to throw themselves away on the divine-demonic figure of the animus in holy-unholy shamelessness, like a Babylonian temple *hierodule* (holy slave). The insight that the virtue of modesty is necessary for women in regard to the archetypal figure of the spirit can be granted her only by an act of grace from the pneuma, if she cannot be reached by the moderating counsel of well-wishing friends.

We recall that the dark angel of the seventh scene bears feminine features. It is the *feminine* aspect of Dionysus (who of course has essentially a double-sexed character) which stands in the foreground, and indeed, this is as women experience him. At the same time, the underworld that is the abyss of the creative power, which was symbolized in the veiled phallus of this scene, has transformed itself in the person of the angel into the divine sympathy of Sophia, whose punishment and reprimand signify an act of higher love. A figure like the feminine pneuma in the seventh scene is dark and productive of fear for the woman because it far exceeds her power of conscious comprehension. It rushes upon her like a gale of wind or like the wings of a bird whirring down in order to mediate to her the "amazing light of self-learned wisdom," as Philo of Alexandria expressed it – namely, that the true love of the woman, even her love for the spirit, is a profanation without a sense of modesty.

For men, the problem of modesty as a virtue belonging to inner development arises on another level, namely, on the natural level, as represented by the symbolic associations of the third scene – the fauns and young goats in the rocky forest. The Titanic greed of men must first of all be educated and purified into a sense of modesty toward the divinity of *nature*. In the spiritual sphere, where men are inherently more conscious than women, they are likely to have the necessary sense of modesty of their own accord. By this, of course, I do not mean the intellect, which is always immodest as long as it does not acknowledge anything higher than itself. I mean the spirit as a primeval phenomenon, in which reason and the irrational are creatively united. Men in whom this spirit achieves effectiveness often have a natural shyness about exposing the results of their creative activity carelessly or openly. They frequently express themselves hesitantly or in complicated ways, in order never by any means to lay violent hands on the secrets of the autonomous spirit. We might think, for example, of the philosopher Kant and his extremely difficult language. This is a sign of his exceptional spiritual reserve. Or we might think of the protective distinction with which Goethe has left the arcana of his inner drama as a legacy to the world, veiled under the cloak of high and individual art in part two of *Faust*.

On the contrary, women, like the eternal little kid, may not perhaps find in themselves the corresponding shy reserve toward the animus and the secrets of the creative spirit. For them, spiritual modesty is embodied in the angel figure of a pneuma, which psychologically speaking can be described as their superordinate personality or – in the sense of Jung and Kerényi – as the *"divine maiden."*[53] Of course the divine maiden by no means always appears in so pure and high a figure as on our frescoes.[54] When a woman considers herself as too pure, too good, or too harmless, the divine maiden can also take on witch-like features. The divine maiden always presents the image of what the woman is not and about which she knows nothing. If the woman becomes witch-like, as occurs in the case of the animus-possession and corresponding inflation, then the divine maiden appears as an embodiment of divine, dark purity. Generally speaking, the divine maiden symbolizes the purely feminine sphere of experience, which always remains foreign to the man and to which he never finds admission, simply because he is a man and therefore totally different from a woman.

In exact correspondence, a woman certainly has no access to the purely masculine sphere of experience either. When a woman cherishes the notion that she can understand a man through and through, into the furthest corner of his heart, as is unfortunately often the case, this is a delusion that arises from the animal need for the closeness of the little kid, and it only too often leads to very real violations by her. In a corresponding delusion, a woman can also fall victim to the image of the animus, and then it is just as devastating. The animus also, being a masculine image, is totally different from her femininity.

The sexes, both as realities and as symbols, are akin to one another in a brotherly-sisterly way, or in a nuptial way, and, as man and woman, can make a pair. Yet certainly they are at the same time primeval opposites, eternally divided; they stand always diametrically opposed to one another. If one is light, then the other is dark, and vice versa; if the spirit of one is like the sun, then the spirit of the other is like the moon. In the matriarchal order of society, in archaic morning time, the antithesis between man and woman was very much in the foreground. In classical antiquity, it still played a significant part in the great feminine mystery cults such as Eleusis, for example. Nevertheless, the more the woman emancipates herself, as was the case in the Rome of the Emperors and again today, the more the primeval antithesis of the sexes is wiped out through the common increase of consciousness; and then there arises the frightful danger that a woman may lay violent hands not only on the sphere of men, but also directly on the creative spirit. In the experience of the spirit, the woman always stands in the *passive* role. She must preserve her maidenly reserve, lest she sound her own feeling and the superordinate personality in herself as well.

The Eighth Scene

We come now to the eighth scene, which is connected with the seventh through the central symbol of the angel, common to both. In the eighth scene, the gaze of the angel is directed upon the first woman's figure, and it is against her that the angel raises the whip, intending to strike. But the eighth scene no longer runs along the short wall of the chamber, but along the long outer wall which has a window in the middle.

In our discussion of the fifth scene, we have tried to show that the events portrayed on the short wall (around the commanding picture of Dionysus and Ariadne) point to events in an innermost sanctuary. What is portrayed on the two long walls appears, on the contrary, to point to events in an outer sanctuary or in a vestibule. Psychologically speaking, we can say that the short back wall corresponds to the sphere of the collective unconscious insofar as it is approachable to human beings in the symbolism of religious rites; the vestibule of the place of mystery corresponds rather to a personal sphere. In any case, we are concerned here with events in which consciousness has a direct part.

In the eighth scene, the angel dashes out invisibly, so to speak, from concealment in the mystery chamber, governed by God himself, into the personal sphere. Now the Dionysian pneuma seizes the initiate. The initiate is the first figure of the eighth scene, and here again she is represented as kneeling. But how greatly she has changed! Everything stiff, all lifeless doll-likeness, has disappeared. Inwardly animated, almost divinely beautiful in her deep despair, she has cast herself down and laid her head, with loosened hair, in the lap of the priestess who sits behind her, unreservedly surrendering herself to her own abasement. She has been cast out of the innermost sanctuary, and now she is cut off from everything with which she was once united. After she was torn away from her manifold relatedness to the world – as we showed in the fourth scene in connection with the so-called terrified woman – she now appears to have also lost her relationship to the soul-image and thus to the spirit. No symbol for the animus is to be seen near her; he is no longer there. But in place of this loss, she has gained something: first, the support of the priestess whom, in the seventh scene, she had still heedlessly rejected; and second, her natural humanity. She is completely alive in her moving, hopeless pain. And now, when she is entirely desperate and thus entirely redeemed – now the Dionysian holy ghost strikes her with its blow. The enthusiastic, puffed-up seeress of the seventh scene has been rejected by the invading pneuma. But the dark angel looks upon the unhappy woman in her true human pain. To judge by the representation, the initiate herself appears not to see the angel. Her eyes are no longer too wide open; they are lowered in modesty and fear. But the priestess who sits behind her looks upon the pneuma. She too is terrified, but she can endure it and calmly perform her office. She has laid her left hand in motherly protection upon the disheveled hair of the initiate, and with the right she pushes the drapery over her back a little to the side, so that the angel may really strike her. She does not speak nor does she herself take any part; she only sees to it that the governance of the pneuma is not impeded.

As I said earlier, the stroke of the pneuma's whip has been interpreted by certain scholars as a flagellation, and thus as a torture. It seems to me that this cannot be the correct meaning. When the eighth scene begins, the angel has already punished the initiate; the chastisement lay in the alienation from the angel, in her warding-off gesture against the initiate in the seventh scene. The despairing woman of the eighth scene is the initiate who is already, *before* the blow, suffering under chastisement from the angel. That the angel has cut her off from the divine, which seemed to her already within reach – that is her torture. The racked feeling of unworthiness and helpless destitution with which she has cast herself into the lap of the priestess is her chastisement. The angel's blow, which reaches her here in this truly frightful situation, is certainly no torture; it is, on the contrary, *forgiveness* which meets her here as the blinding light of self-learned wisdom. Only when she herself is nothing can she receive everything; then, through the whiplash of the Dionysian spirit, she is *redeemed*. If we may use a comparison, which I admit is pretty lame, the blow of the pneuma might correspond to a knightly dubbing; it makes the initiate a definitely initiated person and carries her "as with one blow" to the goal of the initiation.

The prerequisite for this, if we may say it in a single word, is that she must *differentiate* herself–or must be differentiated–from everything that she is not. In this respect, the initiation way invariably has a double meaning. It always presents relationship and, at the same time, differentiation. While relationship with god-filled nature was first established for the initiate (in the third scene), she was at the same time differentiated from her world and its Titanic greed. And then in the *katabasis,* when she took up relationship with the spirit-filled realm of the dead, she was at the same time differentiated from the nature-like manifestations of her earthly Eros. She died to everything in which she as a woman had been entangled. She revived in the drama of imagination through which the guiding spirit preceded her like a torch, but then she was differentiated also from this guiding spirit through the descent of the pneuma.

The initiate of the Orphic mysteries, therefore, always goes through the same double process which is expressed again and again in the Indian wisdom of the *Upanishads,* for example, by two sentences that complete one another. One sentence reads *tat tvam asi*–"that thou art"–and the other, *neti, neti,* which may be translated "that thou art not." Now in the eighth scene, the initiate has reached a point where she has experienced everything that she is *not,* where nothing remains to her but the feeling of terrible destitution and overpowering remorse for the profanation that is represented in the seventh scene. But this profanation was, after all, by no means the first. Where people are unconscious, they always transgress. As long as a woman is identified with the world, she lays violent hands on it; as long as she is identified with the principle of relatedness, she lays violent hands on people and things; and as long as she is identified with the animus, she lays violent hands on the spirit. The constantly repeated declaration *neti, neti,* that thou art not, is an essential aspect of becoming conscious. The undifferentiated state of the unconscious person is brought to an end through the staggering insight that a deficiency of differentiation signifies, at the same time, a shamelessness and a profanation. This is the most decisive and most basic inner knowledge that the initiate receives upon the mystery way.

At the same time, however, she is absolutely cast by force into her deepest reality, namely, into her own femininity. The ambiguous and dangerous animation of sexuality represented in the seventh scene had really been only a preparation for what the feminine in its entire range could reveal to her – what could break in upon her as Sophia (who also, of course, the initiate is not). Sophia, however, directs her, as by a blow from a whip, into the boundaries of her *own* femininity, so that she may remain in control of herself and respect the masculine spirit, not only in men but also in herself. Then the initiate, who in the seventh scene was so ugly, is filled with true beauty. It is as though the painter wished to, or had to, represent the fact that a human being who stands entirely in her own deepest psychic reality, and in nothing else, is also truly beautiful.

According to the representation in our frescoes, if a woman is to learn to stand firm in her feminine reality, it seems necessary that she completely accept another woman and give her her trust, as our initiate does when she casts herself into the lap of the priestess who sits behind her. This step comes so late in our initiation way and is enforced by so terrible a calamity that we must conclude that we are concerned here with something extraordinarily difficult. Even in the seventh scene, the initiate had not been able to accept the counsel of the priestesses with their little basket. At that time she had obviously still thought that she could accomplish it alone, or could accomplish it by relying on the symbol of the ecstatic Silenus, or on the guiding symbol of the animus; everything must crash about her before another woman can finally be helpful to her. This is something that must be considered somewhat more closely, for it is certainly not a usual matter.

There are, of course, a great many relationships among women, for every woman on every level of her development needs acceptance not only from men, but also from other women. For this reason, even when they are young, women love to sit together in the ivory tower of their animus opinions and give each other mutual sanction for these opinions. They converse then with love and with dignity – each a lovable Livia. They love very much too sometimes to join together into a flock of little kids and be submissively edified by how marvelous the music of the spheres sounds and how musical they all are. Even in their genuine experience of the animus, they need the acceptance of other women; each carefully approves the lighted torch of the others. Nevertheless, all such relationships are distinguished by a greater or lesser purposefulness. Moreover, when all is said and done, the women do not reveal themselves to one another – or only exactly as far as is necessary for a certain purpose.

This happens not because they do not *want* to reveal themselves to one another. It happens because they simply cannot do it, at least not in the Western world. Since ancient times, occidental development has been stamped above all by the masculine spirit, and the feminine essence has found only a restricted place in it. Already in ancient Greece, expressions of primal femininity unrelated to the man, which characterized archaic matriarchy, were restricted to the privacy of cults as a holy-unholy secret. Christianity then buried under heavy layers of rejection everything feminine that was not fitted to the requirements of the man. Only the symbol of motherliness of the purified Christian mold was cultivated as an ideal which individual women could strive for. The femininity of women could feel secure only in a cautiously cleared little Garden of the Virgin, its only legitimate abode.

Naturally, there existed along with this the most varied, typical forms of feminine relationship to men and to society. Toni Wolff once tried to present these types in an essay; in it she called attention to the types of the *hetaira,* the *mediumistic woman* and the *Amazon,* in addition to the type of the *mother.*[55] However, all of these are types of feminine relatedness to men and to society; this is the case even with the type of the Amazon. It is the relatedness to men and to society which gives the relatedness its direction, even if in a negative sense. The Amazon, so to speak, is the type of emancipated woman who existed before there were masculine forms of culture. The Amazon rejects men only in order to appropriate their cultural forms for herself. A contemporary form of the Amazon, for example, is what one might call the "boyish type" which, it seems to me, appears quite frequently among modern girls. Here one can best see how emancipation, which is stressed in this type with all its independence, is still turned exclusively toward masculine cultural forms.

These types are all in a certain sense one-sided, precisely because they represent only various possibilities of a woman's relatedness to men and society. Because of this one-sidedness, they all cast a dark shadow, in which a corresponding unrelatedness comes to expression as negative. We know this best in regard to the type of the mother, which is the most familiar to the person molded by Christianity. Freud captured the shadow of motherliness precisely in the concept of the "terrible mother." Corresponding shadow images belong also to the other types. To the hetaira type, for example, who considered positively is the loving one toward men, belongs as symbol of the shadow the type of the prostitute in whom love seems to be destroyed. To the type of the mediumistic woman, who relates herself in a genuine way to the psychic background of men and society, belongs as shadow those bad mediums who only stir up dust or carry on completely black magic. And to the Amazon type, in whose emancipation a genuine necessity for development can appear, belongs as shadow the despotic rule of unmitigated matriarchy.

None of these types can give us an impression of how it looks when a woman rests purely and solidly upon her femininity; none can give us an indication of what this can mean. In our Pompeiian mystery cult, however, we have an archetypal image of the deepest significance for just this femininity resting entirely upon itself. Perhaps it is too simple to say it is Ariadne, for that would not be exactly right, for, of course, the symbol of pure femininity complete in itself is the *forsaken Ariadne-Persephone on Naxos*. Only this forsaken Ariadne, who is entirely alone in the divine seclusion of the island–only she is the mother-bride of the divine father-bridegroom.

We should remind ourselves here briefly that the Ariadne myth relates that she was either slain by Artemis upon Naxos or she hanged herself in despair over her guilt. As I also said earlier, Hofmannsthal represented these mythical associations in his drama *Ariadne on Naxos* in the fact that Ariadne yearns only for death and, when Dionysus approaches, believes he is death and casts herself into its arms. The forsaken Ariadne on Naxos is really a dead woman; and for this reason she is here synonymous also with Persephone, the ruler of the dead. It is a profound symbol which shows that a woman is pure in her femininity at just that moment when she dies entirely to herself.

The Ariadne symbolism shows also the strikingly deep relation of femininity to death. Femininity fulfills itself not in the life of nature, not in the life of the spirit, but in rebirth through death, as is symbolized in the myth of the forsaken Ariadne. On the archaic and primitive level, of course, the deep connection between the feminine principle and death is seen in projection, on account of which women always play a particular part at deaths – for example, as bearers of the lamentation for the dead. In the lamentation, the woman can express rebirth through death untiringly and fully for the entire tribal society; here she is in her true element, for in this she is herself completely fulfilled. This was also so in the times of antiquity. In Rome, for example, legislators attempted again and again to restrain women's public lamentations for the dead, which were among the noisiest festivities, but they never succeeded. The lamentation for the dead can sometimes become a lasting mode of existence for women. This is represented as a prototype in the story of Niobe. One might say a great deal more about this phenomenon. It is expressed in all times and on all cultural levels, as in the quite intimate relationship which unconscious women who are in bondage to nature can have to those who have died, so that these may become more important to them than the living.

The same phenomenon finds very remarkable expression in the myth of Pasiphaë, in which the primal matriarchal order of society appears in its earthly paradisaical innocence. Minos, Pasiphaë's husband, plays hardly any part in the myth as long as he is alive. Any completely unknown bull of the sun can mate with Pasiphaë as well as he; when she bears the Minotaur, the bull has already disappeared again. He too is not important. Minos himself does not achieve any significance after he has begotten with Pasiphaë the two human daughters, Ariadne and Phaidra. Only when he is *dead* does his figure grow to true greatness; together with his brother, he becomes a judge of the dead in the underworld, and then only, as a dead man, is he the equal partner of the eternally living Pasiphaë.

At the end of his piece in *Essays on a Science of Mythology,* Jung says that in a matriarchal order of society men are an indispensable but, on the whole, disturbing factor. This matriarchy corresponds with the primeval condition of feminine earthiness. A certain consciousness must dawn before the woman can recognize the man as a living partner and follow him for further development of consciousness. But even then a man, as a living being, can again become a disturbing factor. This is portrayed in the myth of Pasiphaë's daughter Phaidra, who follows Theseus on the road to Athens and there becomes his queen. But when her own feminine life breaks through again in her blind instinct-driven love for Hippolytus, Theseus continues to play a role for her only insofar as she can use him in a matriarchal way; otherwise he is no longer important. And with awakened femininity, death too erupts in her: as soon as she sees herself crossed, she kills herself without hesitation, because then her only possibility for fulfillment is in actual death.

In the story of Medea, which I also told earlier, the development is similar. There the motif of projection stands completely in the foreground. First of all, Medea projects upon Jason the image of the rescuing hero; then she projects all guilt on him, even her own. She kills him and all her children in order to experience her own fulfillment in projected form through these dead people and in all the death which she, as black magician, scatters far and wide.

The myths of the feminine figures who originate from the family of the great old Helios symbolize levels of development of femininity, some part of which every woman can contain in herself, in her own person and in her own way. Even a woman living today may pass through a phase in which she, like an archaic matriarch, feels the man as a disturbing factor; this may be because he has robbed her of her maidenhood, or because she has borne children, or because her unconscious earthiness has been disturbed in some other way by masculine influences. She will then react with uncanny resistances against a particular man or against men in general. Such women experience their femininity as something completely passive, which it surely is in a certain sense; they forget that they themselves also have consciousness and become active through it, and therefore were and are men's collaborators in everything that occurs. Like Medea, many women living today can, under some conditions, also project all the guilt of the world upon men. So it comes about, for example, that the real injustice inflicted upon women in the Christian Middle Ages is still perpetuated with real bitterness by more than a few women today, when it has long been made good. Death moves in the neighborhood of modern women too in all such cases, certainly not (needless to say) with the monumental power of the old myths, but yet with the same significance, namely, of striving for fulfillment outwardly, instead of in their own inner being.

In contrast, the Ariadne myth leads beyond this whole problem. The forsaken Ariadne on Naxos, as I said earlier, bears also the name Aridela, meaning "she who has become clear." What becomes clear on Naxos first of all is Ariadne's own guilt. In the Ariadne myth this does not appear in projection; it is suffered through, on Naxos, and expiated by death. Then it becomes clear that in this death the heroine becomes a goddess: forsaken by all life, she is as great as the underworld Persephone. So Ariadne, when dead, is the embodiment of the feminine principle in and for itself. The wise woman in alchemy is a true counterpart of her image. While the red man, her brother and bridegroom, bears the warm color of life, she appears in the cold, ghostly color of death. Likewise, she often brings death, for example, in the alchemical fable of Arisleus and Beja found in *Psychology and Alchemy.*

Jung's essay contains a modern dream which elucidates the Ariadne symbolism very aptly. I will quote just the end. The dream concerns a dancer, who changes herself during the dance into the most varied forms. Always dancing on, she is ". . . now naked, and even tears the skin from her body, and finally falls down – a naked skeleton. This is buried, but at night a lily grows out of the grave, and from its cup there rises a *white lady*, who floats slowly up to the sky."[56]

Here we have the same transformation and clarification as in the myth of Ariadne, who on Naxos may also be called one who is buried. The naked skeleton is a terrifying image, but when one observes it objectively it is of great significance. The skeleton of a human being is his most indestructible part; it can survive for hundreds – even thousands – of years, intact. It is also the part that gives the body its typical form and solidity. The skeleton is, therefore, the indestructible and form-giving part of the human being. A dead person who is at the same time alive is a similar symbol. One who is already dead cannot die any more, and when he becomes divinely alive in death, like Ariadne, he has achieved a lasting, unchangeable life. The naked skeleton, or the dead person who still lives, is an indestructible, eternal figure, which cannot be harmed by the changes of life. The ideas of eternal indestructibility, of form-giving and of solidity-bestowing power – these are all ideas which belong to the archetypal symbol of the Self. The symbols of the naked skeleton and of the divine, living dead are consequently outer shapes of the Self. The forsaken Ariadne, as she reveals herself on Naxos as a dead woman, is the embodiment of the feminine principle which, in the *conjunctio* with the masculine principle, makes up the totality of the Self. The same is represented in the alchemical *conjunctio*. In the Ariadne myth we see how, in the moment when the feminine principle reveals itself, it is already no longer alone; Dionysus, in this case the embodiment of the masculine principle, unites himself with it in holy marriage and then, so says the myth, the wine flows.

The Indian couple of Shiva and Shakti offers a parallel to Dionysus and Ariadne in their union on Naxos. I refer here again to the lovely Roman relief of the marriage on Naxos[57] which may be compared, without further ceremony, with pictures of Shiva and Shakti. In the case of the Indian pair, the masculine symbol carries the character of death; Shiva is a god of death, Shakti is life. In the case of the union of Dionysus and Ariadne, both are at the same time death and life. This mythical representation is very interesting for us because it shows that, on the feminine side, death must break through first as the last fulfillment. In myths which mainly correspond to masculine psychology, the reverse is the case. Death appears as a process in the archetypal masculine realm. An example of this is the myth of Osiris.

In this case, what does the symbol of death mean? Death stands opposed to all human life and is the very thing of which in reality human beings can discern nothing. Death is forever on the other side of the boundary which is set for consciousness; it is an eternally impenetrable mystery. As opposed to the consciousness of the living, death symbolizes the mystery of the unconscious psyche, which contains in itself the unifying symbol as center – the Self. In the Self all opposites – masculine and feminine, death and life – are together in incomprehensible completeness. The symbol of this unification lives like a promise in the souls of all people; everywhere and at all times it is produced by the imagination as a solace in the vicissitudes of life and as an image of the goal.

To return again to the figure of Ariadne, she is for a woman the image of the goal. But at the same time, she portrays the way to the goal, which flows into death; that is to say that the way moves into a situation where consciousness – and especially everything personal that women take as so surpassingly important – no longer plays a role at all. It is really this condition which women long for when they occupy themselves so intently with problems of death, with the remembrance of those who have died, or with ideas about life after death. Something in them always longs to find itself where the personal no longer plays a part. That is Death, whom they already greet with foreboding in the transitoriness of the world, for something in them senses that then the wine will begin to flow. What was formerly unbridgeable opposition between the light of day and the gloom of night intermingles in this death to a blessed dusk, out of which the god sends forward a small, earnest Silenus – a gnome, a helpful spirit – with a drop of sweet wine. All problems are resolved because no more solutions can be sought by consciousness. Life then comes forth entirely out of the unconscious psyche as the fragrant breath of the Self.

According to the Orphic view, a woman who strives for this redemption – from the personal, one may say – must go the way which the god, the prototype, has set as an example for her. It is thus represented in the frescoes of the Villa of Mysteries, but in an unexpected way. In the beginning, the fate of Zagreus is the prototype; the death and the rebirth of Dionysus are relived by the initiate. But in the decisive moment of the seventh scene, where everything hangs by a thread, the prototype changes unexpectedly. The coming down of the Dionysian pneuma really saves the initiate by pointing out that the feminine prototype is now leading the way.

Enlightened and overcome by this penetrating wisdom, the initiate follows this prototype, and in the eighth scene she, like Ariadne, has reached her Naxos.

In this connection, one can ask oneself what it was that actually overcame her or how it might look in reality when the Dionysian pneuma sets an Orphic initiate right. Naturally we know nothing about this; we can only express a conjecture which seems conceivable from a psychological standpoint. When opposites are unified in the symbol of the Self that has succeeded in becoming effective, then not only are life and death reconciled, but reality and psychological reality as well. Then the outer and the inner are no longer experienced as realms alien to one another. One might therefore conjecture that the initiate has experienced something in the inflation which is represented in the seventh scene or, to put it better, that something has happened to her that is like a *casus ab alto* – to quote Jung's words from his essay "Concerning the Self" – through which her puffed-up-ness has been reduced. From a psychological standpoint, this seems plausible. The "redemption" – or, to put it in modern terms, the becoming a Self – is actually something that one cannot win simply through diligent imagining nor through deeply burrowing introversion. Whenever the Self comes into being, things happen outside and inside at the same time; not only the person, but also his life situation – everything – changes. The Dionysian holy ghost descends not only on the heads, or at best the hearts, of human beings; he moves in nature and even in lifeless things; *he is psychic reality,* which is experienced simultaneously both without and within.

Accordingly, it seems probable that something has happened to the initiate between the seventh and the eighth scenes, something that was like a *casus ab alto.* How small or how great the corresponding occurrence may have been can naturally not be known; however, it does not matter. The smallest happening can bring everything about, if people can let themselves be impressed by its meaningfulness.

The Naxos of the initiate, then, is the outer sanctuary where the priestess receives her. That the fulfillment of the initiate takes place here and not in the innermost sanctuary is strikingly symbolic of the fact that the mystery initiation can come to a conclusion only in the initiate's own reality. Consciousness must be joined to inner events, and the conscious individual must take part in them with full responsibility. But this is a terribly difficult step; it includes allowing the most hidden thoughts to become manifest (the symbol for this is the loosened hair), and the experience of remorse, shame, and also despair that the past is dead and can never again be alive. The condition of forsakenness and death, which is like the Naxos of Ariadne, involves also the inexorable renunciation of all wishes which the woman once cherished, of all longings which had been dear to her, of all striving that has given her wings. It is truly a parting from everything personal. This parting she must experience in the personal sphere of the outer sanctuary, because she personally must take it seriously and accept it as binding. To this death she must now say, "That am I."

Certainly a woman could not take this difficult step alone. She must know that there are women who have gone before her and who can therefore fully appreciate her difficult position at this moment. In the eighth scene this role is played by the priestess into whose lap the initiate has cast herself. This is the third woman's figure which embodies, with the initiate, a relationship between one woman and another of religious character; this relationship is not determined by conscious intent, nor does it serve a mutual approbation.

The first such religious woman was the priestess of the first scene, in whose presence the initiate was taught the *theoria* of the cult. This one therefore was a teacher. But she does not teach the initiate *personally* and does not impart any knowledge of her own. She only takes care that the initiate should correctly receive the message of the god conveyed through the myth. The second religious woman of this kind was the principal priestess of the second scene. Through her higher motherliness as representative of Cybele, she shows the initiate the way—leading indeed not upward, but downward into the divinity of nature. She opens for her the way which has been given to every woman by her own religious instinct. She, like the first priestess, is not personally related to the initiate; she has before her eyes not the initiate, but the way. Now as we already said, the priestess of the eighth scene embodies the woman who has gone before the initiate to the goal of the initiation and can fully appreciate her situation. But she too does this in an entirely impersonal way. She only covers the confusion of the initiate with the cloak of love; that is, she lays her hand on the disheveled hair of her ward. She does not look at the initiate, but at the Dionysian pneuma, and receives her guidance from there. She does not try to enter into the feelings of the suffering woman in a feminine way or to understand her, for that is something that no one can do.

The essential proceedings of an initiation are truly archetypal phenomena, but nevertheless every single person experiences them in so individual a way that other people can at most, by a hint, mediate how they themselves have had similar experiences. The priestess of the eighth scene does this in a very remarkable and modest way. For now *she* wears the same cap as the kneeling woman of the seventh scene, and she has a staring expression in her eyes similar to that of the kneeling woman, though indeed less strongly emphasized. This means that the priestess shows the sufferer through her appearance that she has gone through the *same mistakes* as the poor, kneeling penitent. She is like her, for she too is one who has received a blow. By showing herself in her erring humanity, she becomes a solace and help to the initiate. She precedes her, not through superiority, but as one who has submitted with her, before her.

A figure similar to this priestess of the eighth scene is found in the metamorphoses of Apuleius.[58] After the mystagogue Lucius has been inducted into the mysteries of Isis, he receives in a dream the directive to look for a priest and discovers him as a lame man with a terribly dislocated foot. The one who can best mediate to the mystagogue Lucius is therefore one who has once gone too far and who has had a fall. According to the view of this ancient mystery, therefore, the individual who is the most mature is not one who has superior knowledge and does right and is good; rather, it is the one who has learned, from ignominious mistakes, religiously to extract the right experience, at the right time and in the right place.

According to the representation of our fresco series, the initiate finds her own feminine reality through trial and error; thereby she follows the prototype of Ariadne, and through it she, like Ariadne, has found her Naxos. With this, she stands now entirely in feminine darkness; for us this has become a strange, even repulsive, idea because of the mantle of heavenly light around the Virgin Mary. In order to find an objective example for feminine darkness, we must turn as far as China, where the feminine is also seen as dark, but without negative valuation. It is described there as *Yin* or the shadow side of the mountain.

Ariadne corresponds to this too, for she is not a bright figure. She is the dark daughter of Pasiphaë and, even in becoming clear, she remains dark. She is not a heavenly ruler like the Virgin Mary. Her figure reaches even the labyrinthine depth of the Minotaur, who is her half-brother. Therefore she is also the dark form of Dionysus, familiar with the bull-god from the beginning. One has to keep these associations in mind, because otherwise one misunderstands the figure of Ariadne-Persephone on Naxos, idealizing her in the Christian sense. Ariadne is not a higher but, on the contrary, *a lower ideal.* It is essential for the understanding of our frescoes that just the depth which she embodies is the place of fulfillment and redemption for the initiate of the Orphic cult.

In a secret way Ariadne, as daughter of Pasiphaë and sister of the Minotaur, is very closely related to the modest figure of Baubo, as the latter appears in Eleusis. The earthiness which makes Ariadne dark is humanized in the figure of Baubo and therefore irradiated by a racy humor. When the humor of Baubo flashes comfortingly out before the sorrowing Demeter, there is a Dionysian fulfillment and healing, whose counterpart in the Ariadne myth is the epiphany of the wine. The feminine depth which appears to be personified in Ariadne as well as in Baubo, as soon as it becomes clear, is vibrant and causes others to vibrate with it. It is this vibration the spirit approaches; he presses himself to it. In the dark principle of the feminine form, the creative, masculine principle finds self-realization.

The vibrance which wells up from the feminine depth as fulfillment and healing declares itself in the eighth scene of the

Pompeiian fresco series in the striking change from the first two to the last two figures. The third and fourth figures of the eighth scene are both in complete vibration. A nude woman stretches herself upward, dancing and floating. She turns her back on the onlooker while a beautifully dressed woman, who looks into the Initiation Chamber, circles about the nude one with a *thyrsus* in her hand.

These two figures have been interpreted by all scholars as the representation of a *deificatio* – that is, a deification – such as forms the conclusion in many ancient mystery cults, through which the mystagogue appeared as honored and raised to divine splendor. In this way the end of the initiation is represented also in Apuleius – for example, where the initiated Lucius, "as when a statue is unveiled, dressed like the sun," stands before the people.[59] In this sense it is quite certainly correct to explain the two last figures of the eighth scene as deification. But it is a question what or who thereby appears deified. In order to understand this, we must rely on the teaching of the Orphic initiation cult, about which, in this respect, there is no misunderstanding. The goal of the Orphic mystery cult is, of course, not deification of the human being. It consists of the definitive liberation of the Dionysian spark, which is the immortal soul of the human being, and in its union with Dionysus. Accordingly, one must understand the nude, aspiring figure in the eighth scene as a symbol for the divine spark in the initiate which, having just been freed by the blow of the Dionysian pneuma, prepares to soar upward to achieve union with the god. This interpretation finds confirmation in the fact that the aspiring figure is entirely nude, that is, entirely divine, for in antiquity, nudity is an attribute of the divine. That the aspiring figure turns her back to the onlooker is also very significant; it means that she is indeed to be sensed in outline, but nevertheless remains impenetrable, as indeed, the divine is always impenetrable to the human being. The hovering figure embodies rather a hope than a certainty; with her upraised arms she indicates mainly the *direction* which leads to union with the god. At the same time she clashes the Dionysian cymbals in her upraised hands and thereby beats the time or the rhythm for the woman's figure which revolves around her. This figure of the beautifully dressed woman with the *thyrsus,* gazing into the world with a strangely absent glance – she, I believe, is an *embodiment of the initiate* who has found redemption and has learned to know the way which will be right for her, even beyond death.

If we keep before our eyes the fact that, at the end of the initiation the divine figure of Ariadne is a prototype for the initiated, so too we dare not fail to draw on the Ariadne myth to understand the two last figures. In this myth there is, at the end, a symbol that contributes a great deal to the understanding of the nude figure, and that is the *crown* of Ariadne, which Dionysus gives to his beloved at the very beginning and, after the wedding on Naxos, removes to heaven in memory of her. We discussed this symbol at the appropriate time and have seen that the crown signifies the Self as it was innate in human beings from the very beginning; but it remains latent (unconscious) until it is made conscious through a process of development.

According to this meaning, the nude figure of the eighth scene as a symbol for the human immortal soul corresponds to the symbol of the crown of Ariadne. The immortal in human beings is that which crowns them – which lends them dignity, value, and meaning; which makes their lives worth living from the very beginning, even when they do not know it at all. Immortality signifies indestructibility, permanence, firmness; it signifies everything that characterizes the Self, which is the origin of the human being; and when it becomes conscious, it appears as the goal around which consciousness revolves. This goal hovers constantly in front of consciousness, as the nude figure hovers constantly in front of the revolving mystagogue and as the starry crown hovers in front of Ariadne – for her remembrance, as the myth says, as that which she dare never forget. The end of initiation is reached when this goal hovers in front of consciousness as direction-giving; the human being is "released" when she is no longer bound to anything else, no longer related to anything else but this goal. Then she is one who is twice-born; her life now becomes a real life, one that has meaning, exactly because it has a goal. Such a person then becomes a true human being, as she recognizes the central point within herself – and above her – about which she revolves.

It is interesting that, at the moment when the initiation is at an end, a masculine symbol appears again (in the eighth scene of the fresco series). I refer to the *thyrsus* which the initiated one carries during her revolving, forward movement. We have already spoken about the *thyrsus*–a hollow staff which, according to myth, was filled with Dionysian fire. The *thyrsus* is a symbol similar to the torch of the seventh scene, but in this case the fire does not appear outside, but hidden, even firmly shut away inside. Above all, the *thyrsus* is not an instrument of torture, like the *extinguished* torch. It is light, delicate, unobtrusive; it indicates that, as an initiated one, its bearer belongs to the god and that through him she has found her way to a true life. Like the torch, the *thyrsus* of the eighth scene is also an animus symbol which now, however, the initiated one has in her hand. To translate this symbolism quite simply, we can perhaps say that the initiated one, whose feminine depth has become clear, knows from this depth how to deal with the animus. In her the animus is no longer autonomous. He has become a function, as we may perhaps express it according to modern psychological language: he has become an element contained within the completeness of the woman, that revolves with her around the goal. Then the spiritual development of the woman is no longer the goal; it *serves* the goal.

When the Orphic initiation reaches its end successfully, everything becomes simple and few words are needed. As soon as the feminine depths have been reached, the way to the light opens also and all complications and uncertainties vanish. Yet at the same time, everything becomes mysterious, just as the initiated person herself becomes a mystery. This we can gather from her mysterious glance, as though she were withdrawn, as she gazes out into the world. Her grave, composed expression indicates an intensification which in everything seeks the One, which finds the god even as she finds the world. In the way she gazes and moves, one could describe the initiated one as an embodiment of centeredness. This is indeed an unlovely word, but it nevertheless indicates the psychological attitude which is arrived at through initiation.

As we have seen, the eighth scene consists of two parts, which we had to observe separately in order to understand something of the meaning. Maiuri, however, counts both parts as a single scene, and this too is meaningful. The figures of the eighth scene, taken together, represent a quaternity, which consists of three similar figures plus another different figure. From this point of view, one can also interpret the eighth scene as representing the *totality* of the person, in which the three are completed through the addition of the fourth. We may use here also the well-known sentence of Maria Prophetissa that "out of the third comes the one as the fourth."[60] The Self is the one that was indeed always there, but latent; and when it becomes conscious as the fourth – that is, as the goal – it leads the person to wholeness.

I certainly do not believe that it would be permissible to interpret the quaternity of the eighth scene in the sense of the four psychological functions. The function theory is too modern for the ancient initiation picture. Only the principle is usable, that the four correspond with wholeness and that this is experienced as the problem of the three and the fourth, which is of an entirely different nature.

In the eighth scene of our fresco series, this problem appears solved – differently perhaps from in the Cabiri scene from the second part of *Faust,* where the question arises: "*Drei sind's, wo is das Vierte geblieben?*" ("Three there are, where has the fourth tarried?") In our Orphic mystery cult, the myth of Dionysus and Ariadne stands before the initiate as the compelling prototype; and so the way to the fourth is also given to the initiate from the beginning. This is to say that this myth also contains a quaternity. It consists of (1) Dionysus as bull-god, (2) the mortal Ariadne on Crete, (3) the forsaken Ariadne on Naxos, and (4) Dionysus as god of wine.[61]

At this point we might perhaps cast a brief glance back to the representation on the mosaic floor in the North African sanctuary of Dionysus about which we spoke earlier. It originated in the middle of the second century A.D. and is therefore perhaps 150 years later than our frescoes. The fourth side of the mosaic floor corresponds with our seventh fresco scene. It also represents a kneeling Thyiad who is just about to raise the covering from the phallus in the winnowing basket; near her, corresponding with the dark angel, a nymph is floating down with a gesture of modesty. However, the blow which later strikes the feminine figure is here represented in the middle of the floor, separated from this scene. In this case it is not an angel who strikes, but a terrible, demonic, naked man.

The mythical subject for this scene is the legend of the death of the nymph Ambrosia, who was nurse to Dionysus. She was slain by the wild Thracian king Lycurgus with a double axe. According to this representation, the end of the initiation way, therefore, is death. The *deificatio* no longer occurs in this world, but only after death as a redemption through Dionysus, as it is represented, for example, in the history of Semele and many of the Bacchantes. It is interesting that at this later time, when Christian ideas were perhaps already influencing people more strongly, the outcome of the initiation into the outer world stands in the foreground.

To be sure, Dionysus-Isodaites, who invites all people equally unto himself, is also death. He releases people from the suffering of life.

The Ninth and Tenth Scenes

We have now arrived at the end of the way of initiation which is portrayed on the frescoes of the Villa of Mysteries. After the eighth scene, the window of the long outer wall opens, daylight penetrates the room, and the initiated one is again restored to ordinary life. It is generally interpreted in this way by scholars, and certainly this fits. Yet then the conclusion is drawn that the ninth and tenth scenes have no further significance. It is supposed that these pictúres are purely for decoration and represent scenes from the lives of the ladies who lived in the Villa. The lady in the tenth scene is described as the "Domina," because it is thought that this is a portrait of the lady of the house like others which have been found in other houses of antiquity.

These trains of thought start from the very subjective hypothesis that an Orphic initiation might have had a certain significance, but that, after all, ordinary life is entirely meaningless. This is a prejudice that does not belong only to the educated; on the contrary, there are endless numbers of people even today who resign themselves to meaninglessness in ordinary daily life, even at a fairly early age. They have known for a long while that luck is always where they are not. At bottom, this conviction springs from the fact that these people feel themselves to be terribly boring and tedious. They have no confidence in themselves; they make nothing of the gifts which have been given them. Certainly if they had other gifts–if, for example, they were like Mr. X or Mrs. Y –that would be something else again! Then, naturally, they would be highly interesting! But since they are so insignificant, ordinary life can certainly not be other than insignificant too.

To this one can only say that of course all people are very insignificant. Only the goals which they set for themselves have significance. If, for example, a scholar sees his goal only in erudition, perhaps he achieves a certain distinction; but every evening when he looks up from his work he sits, an insignificant man, in surroundings which mean nothing to him.

When the Self arises as goal, however, one's commonality and ordinary life become meaningful. One need no longer wait for the actor's opportunity to play a shining role in the drama of choice or wait for Zeus himself to rain down upon the roof in a shower of gold. The Self is the remedy which makes the whole of life meaningful. Accordingly, the representations of ordinary life in the Villa of Mysteries are naturally meaningful too. It cannot be otherwise, for the people to whom we owe the fresco series did not contrive these pictures by conscious design. The representations are the result of the primordial experience that befell them in this house, and even now it lends a wonderfully fascinating atmosphere. The last two scenes too, with all their simplicity, are highly animated. It will surely reward us, therefore, to look at them with reference to their meaning.

We shall soon see that the end of the initiation certainly does not signify a break. The initiate is not removed either from the experiences that she has just had or from the world. On the contrary, she is reinstated in them anew through the same flow of psychic life that bore her through the initiation.

The ninth scene shows a lady who is in the process of having her hair dressed by a maid. An Eros figure ("cupid") holds a mirror for that purpose, but only the maid looks into it, while the lady gazes thoughtfully into the distance. A second Eros figure behind her looks amiably on.

This picture takes up the still unsolved problem of the eighth scene, namely, the problem of the initiate's hair, which was there disheveled and loose and therefore has to be dressed. As we have already seen, the hair is a symbol for the contents of the head, that is, for all thoughts and ideas that together make up personal consciousness. How these contents of consciousness were really procured is disclosed in the eighth scene, as well as what presuppositions and illusions were mixed up with these contents. However, now all the contents of the head must be put in order in accordance with the new point of view that follows from directing one's goal toward the Self.

The lady, whom we could perhaps describe as a symbol for the ego-personality, looks calmly into the world; she takes up the impressions that come to her from out there. The ordering of the conscious contents follows from the fact that *something* in her, embodied in the maid, glances at the same time into the mirror of the Eros figure. This little winged spirit is surely to be understood as a messenger from the unconscious, who brings to the lady her inner reactions to outer impressions. Objective observation is completed through consideration of subjective emotions. What happens is also regarded as a *mirror of one's own being*. The other little Eros figure represents the quieted Eros of the initiated.

When one directs one's goal toward the Self, the principle of relatedness functions more easily. Relationships to people and things are no longer taken so personally; they moderate themselves, since they also become means to self-knowledge. The difference between outer happenings and inner experience is still only a relative one: life becomes a dream and the dream becomes life, for both are manifestations of the Self.

Consciousness is set in order as it too is recognized as only something relative, dependent upon outer circumstances and inner influences. It has been included in the process of becoming a Self; it can always change again and so must be set in order anew every day with calm impartiality, just as one's hair must be newly dressed every day. In this regard, this or that content can fall away any day as obsolete, and a new content can develop in its place. The human being can no longer boast of omniscience or indisputable truth; what was true yesterday may no longer be true tomorrow. Only the goal is *always* true, about which the human being revolves as a person perpetually in process. It is nice that this condition of relative consciousness or, one might also say, of continual coming to consciousness, is represented in the ninth scene of our fresco series as so friendly and so quiet a condition – as a *composure* which results from confining oneself to immediate circumstance and nothing beyond it. When this composure has been achieved, then entirely ordinary life can become interesting: it is, indeed, new every day, and the individual can take part in it every day in a new way.

If one goes on from this ninth scene in the Initiation Hall of the Villa of Mysteries, one arrives at the great door of the front wall, which leads out to a terrace. From there one's glance travels far over the gently rolling plain which spreads in front of the house. It is supposed that, after the initiation, a banquet may have been held on this terrace. This is certainly possible: the Villa with its many different aspects directly invites one's fantasy to imagine a corresponding life. However this may be, after the ninth scene the prospect opens into God's free nature. The initiated one, who is composed and quieted, can gaze with new eyes at nature too; she can discover therein the mother who smiles upon her from the faces of her children; she can hear the father, who speaks to her in the rustling of the wind. She can let herself be influenced by the peculiar life of animals and plants, which also is like a lovely, meaningful dream. Every day she can thankfully worship the *genius loci* (spirit of place).

Next to the great door we find the tenth little scene, the portrait of a lady, which is the only picture on the front wall. This placement surely indicates that this portrait expresses something unique. The lady, who has been called Domina, is represented as sitting in a comfortable armchair. She is very richly dressed as a distinguished matron. She rests her right arm on a cushion that lies on the arm of the chair. The expression on her face is attentive, and to the left behind her, within her reach, stands a small, oblong, four-cornered object. It might perhaps be that this object is a little writing table such as was customary with the Romans, but this I cannot safely say.

At any rate, this figure of a woman is the only one among the twenty-nine figures of the Initiation Hall which is turned toward the back wall – toward the central picture of Dionysus and Ariadne. The Domina is turned toward this important place of interest and so is connected with it as an *opposite*. This representation leads me to think that the so-called Domina is, very probably, to be interpreted as an embodiment of Mnemosyne – that is, remembrance – which was the most meaningful human faculty for the Orphics.

This was really the most important thing for the future that the participant in the mystery received from the Orphic initiation – namely, she now had something she could always remember. In the dramatic course of the initiation, she has come to know how human life passes to death and over beyond death as a way between height and depth, danger and help – a way which can be trodden according to divine pattern toward a divine goal. The human being who can remember is no longer given over to blind fate. She has, indeed, seen the eternal symbols which in all conditions of life mediate the right demeanor and lend meaning to all events. She has drunk the sweet milk that gushes from the breasts of the Great Mother; she has heard the music of the spheres; the light of bliss has risen before her and the wing-stroke of the pneuma has grazed her. All this is a perpetual reality for the person who remembers it. The picture of the so-called Domina, whether or not it represents the mistress of the house, appears so dominating to me because it embodies Mnemosyne – the "Remembrance" of the Orphics that represents a whole philosophy of life.

The same is true for modern people. In the course of inner development, once the world of archetypal images has arisen in a dramatic, moving inner drama, individuals need never again lose connection with it if they do not forget their most valuable experiences and, with that, themselves.

The *circumambulatio* – which can be experienced by modern people, too, in an inner drama corresponding to the Initiation Hall of the Villa of Mysteries – is only one cycle in the continuous, circular motion of the psyche which, while constantly changing, nevertheless touches on new levels the same stations again and again. Whoever remembers this can always find again a staff and support in the vicissitudes of life. The rhythm of the unconscious psyche carries such people; it becomes alive for them like the beat of the cymbals in the upraised hands of the figure of light, the goal around which they revolve. In this sense, memory is just as important for modern people as it was for the ancient Orphics and also, for example, for Plato. Psychologically speaking, it signifies a concentration upon the essential in connection with everything that happens. This, indeed, is not a matter of course. It requires experience not to let oneself be confused or diverted – if I dare say so – by the arabesques which surround all shapes of life. It requires the gift of remembrance to enable one to seize the basic form in the phantasmagoria of outer and inner happenings, so one can understand the play and participate in it. This concentration upon the essential is expressed in the tenth scene of our fresco series by the attentiveness with which the so-called Domina is turned toward the holy, mystery-filled sphere of the inner wall.

With this, we have completed our reflections upon the fresco series of the Villa of Mysteries. It has signified a daring venture for me, for the only thing upon which I could support myself in this endeavor, as I said in the beginning, was the hypothesis that these frescoes represent a development to which the way of individuation of modern people is a parallel. As we have seen, I tried always to keep this parallel before my eyes and to orient myself by it, step by step. I have at least derived a certain assurance from the fact that this orientation was possible at all. It seems important to me that alchemical parallels to our fresco series could be uncovered again and again; and even if I sometimes could point these out only briefly, they still signify the best corroboration for my initial hypothesis.

What distinguishes the frescoes in the Initiation Hall of the Villa of Mysteries is not only their direct and faithful portrayal of experience, but also the incredibly vast breadth and depth of the treasure of religious ideas which is contained in them. A *lux moderna* dawns in these frescoes – a truly startling light of self-learned wisdom, to quote Philo of Alexandria again. All those buds which in the course of centuries unfolded in Christianity and helped it to victory – all these buds unfolded also in the pictures of the Initiation

Hall of the Villa of Mysteries. But whereas in Christianity the unfolding leads toward the light and the height of the spirit, in our Orphic mystery cult it leads toward the Dionysian depth of the unconscious psyche. For this reason, the Dionysus mystery could not prevail against Christianity. What people needed at the beginning of the Christian era was, first of all, a way out of the limitless thralldom to nature; they needed a *spiritual development* which included also the development and establishment of consciousness. For only a small spiritual elite, such as was obviously gathered in the Villa during one period of time, could the Dionysian cult be meaningful and healing. But now, when again an eon is completed, when the consciousness of people has not only become sufficiently established, but actually rigid, now the *lux moderna* which dawned in the Villa of Mysteries can become healing to mankind. Now it can be glad tidings to many to know that, if the light of the world goes into eclipse, it rises again from the blessed twilight of the unconscious.

Apart from this, the frescoes at the Villa of Mysteries mediate, especially to women, insights which are only rarely found in such abundance. For example, the problems of feminine Eros and feminine spirituality are clarified through the symbolism of the frescoes in an unusually striking and picturesque way. Through the myth of Ariadne and everything connected with it on this feminine initiation way, we are impressively presented with the importance of the way toward underneath, especially for women – how they can find their wholeness only through arriving at the feminine depths. If we dare to believe the representation of our frescoes, a woman, it is true, cannot arrive at this depth through her own strength. It requires an act of grace, which strikes her like the whirring of a dark angel's wings and removes her to the Naxos of the forsaken Ariadne – or, we could also say, to Baubo's hearth.

That it requires grace for a human being to find the place of fulfillment is naturally true not only for women, but also for men. No human being can go the way of becoming a Self without the intervention of super-personal powers. According to the representation of our fresco series, such an intervention is no soothing salve; grace is at the same time punishment, correction, a moral setting straight, despair, forgiveness, all at one stroke. In just this painful way there grows up in forgetful humankind the noble gift of Mnemosyne.

Notes

1. Amadeo Maiuri, *La Villa dei Misteri* (Rome, 1931), is the standard work about everything that concerns the Villa. The entire excavation and all its contents are described in it in every detail, and the exact scientific verification for all opinions or explanations is given. Besides, everything is brought together that has been suggested and published by other research workers about the architectural, artistic, historical, cultish and mythological questions. Since knowledge has not been changed or enriched since then through further discoveries, one can depend on this work in every respect. It contains many beautiful illustrations in text and plates. In 1954 an edition by the Libraria dello Stato appeared with illustrations in color. (There is also a 1947 edition, with a separate portfolio of color illustrations of the frescoes. And beautiful color illustrations of some of the frescoes are found in Amadeo Maiuri, *Roman Painting*, trans. Stuart Gilbert [Geneva: Albert Skira, 1953], pp. 99 ff. – Trans.)

2. Guglielmo Ferrero, *The Women of the Caesars* (New York: Century, 1911).

3. An example might be the so-called younger Agrippina, who was so bitterly maligned by Tacitus, in her lifelong association with the philosopher Seneca. During the rule of Caligula he went with her into exile, and after Nero had murdered her, his mother, he followed her to death, only a few years later. The younger Agrippina was a true follower of Livia, but something was lacking in her: she did not have the same highly reliable discretion.

4. See literature references in Maiuri, *La Villa dei Misteri*. See also an article by Margarete Bieber, "The Mystery Frescoes in the Mystery Villa of Pompeii," *Review of Religion* 2 (November 1937), pp. 3–11. An insert showing photographs of the fresco series is included.

5. Ludwig Friedländer, *Roman Life and Manners* (New York: E. P. Dutton, 1913).

5a. Since published in his volume *Dionysos: Archetypal Image of Indestructible Life*, Bollingen Series 65.2 (Princeton: Princeton University Press, 1976). – Ed.

6. C. G. Jung, *The Collected Works*, Bollingen Series 20, vols. 1–20 (Princeton: Princeton University Press and London: Routledge and Kegan Paul, 1953 ff.), 12, § 34. Hereinafter cited as CW by volume and paragraph numbers.

7. Ibid., § 35.

8. Ibid., §§ 104–05.
9. See, for example, Margaret Murray, *The God of the Witches* (London: Sampson, Low, Marston, n.d.).
10. Diels-Kranz, frag. 15.
11. See Arnold von Salis, *Antike und Renaissance* (1947), plate 56b, opposite p. 177.
12. C. G. Jung, CW 12, § 105n34 (italics added).
13. Compare with this the concept of the *uroboros* in Erich Neumann, *The Origins and History of Consciousness*, trans. R. F. C. Hull, Bollingen Series 42 (Princeton: Princeton University Press, 1954).
14. C. G. Jung, CW 12, § 564 (italics added).
15. Leopold Feiler, *Mysterion* (Vienna: R. M. Rohrer, 1946), pp. 23 ff. A dithyrambic little book, by a doctor who was affected by the frescoes, that contains some valuable allusions and suggestions.
16. H. K. Fierz, *Entwicklungsgeschichte der Chemie* (1945), p. 30.
17. The *lares* were represented by ophites, a variety of marble colored green by serpentine. – Trans.
18. Hans Leisegang, "The Mystery of the Serpent," trans. Ralph Manheim, in *The Mysteries*, Bollingen Series 30.1 (New York: Pantheon Books, 1955), p. 201.
19. Plato, *Symposium or Supper*, trans. Francis Birrell and Shane Leslie (The Nonesuch Press, 1924), p. 88.
20. See, for example, Mircea Eliade's work on Shamanism.
21. See Leopold Feiler, *Mysterion*, p. 29. Here and in what follows I take up various allusions by Feiler.
22. Maiuri, *La Villa dei Misteri*, p. 140.
23. C. G. Jung, CW 12, § 72.
24. C. G. Jung, CW 11, § 317. I refer also to the third chapter of the same essay, in which other than Christian parallels to the transformation mystery are cited.
25. Erwin Rohde, *Psyche*, trans. W. B. Hillis (London: Kegan Paul, 1925), p. 285; also pp. 257 ff. and 282 ff.
26. S. Roscher, *Lexikon der griechischen-römischen Mythologie*, vol. 1, p. 1091, fig. 1.
27. C. G. Jung, CW 13, §§ 239–303. This essay contains alchemical parallels which are of the greatest importance for us (§§ 259–69).
28. A. Dieterich, *Eine Mithras-liturgie,* p. 176.
29. In the original manuscript this paragraph was typed single-spaced. Even though the translator assumed this to be a typist's error, we are acknowledging the difference Linda Fierz-David marked here by setting this in italic. – Ed.
30. C. G. Jung, CW 13, § 263.
31. See in this connection Henri Brémond, *A Literary History of Religious Thought in France*, trans. K. L. Montgomery (1928, 1930). Volume 2, chap. 7, pp. 394 ff. deals with Francois des Sales and Jeanne de Chantal; see also vol. 1, chap. 3, pp. 55–100 with des Sales.
32. C. G. Jung, CW 16, §§ 353–539.

33. Reprinted in J. Jezower, *Buch der Träume* (1938), p. 259.
34. C. G. Jung, CW 12, § 169.
35. Ibid., § 169 (italics added).
36. Ibid., § 171.
37. Ibid., § 173.
38. Ibid.
39. The idea of the "divine fire" in alchemy is parallel. In this connection, see C. G. Jung, CW 13, §§ 256–58.
40. See in this connection Feiler, *Mysterion*, p. 42, where various examples of this are cited.
41. Maiuri, *La Villa dei Misteri*, p. 153.
42. See G. Charles-Picard, *Les religions de l'Afrique antique* (1954), illus. 7.
43. The alchemical idea of Mercurius as spirit of the air is the masculine parallel to this. See C. G. Jung, CW 13, §§ 261 ff.
44. Leisegang, "The Mystery of the Serpent," p. 23.
45. Ibid., pp. 203 ff.
46. Ibid., pp. 78 ff.
47. See in this connection Paul Francois Foucart, *Les Mystères d'Eleusis* (Paris, 1914).
48. See in this connection Franz Cumont, *The Oriental Religions in Roman Paganism* (New York: Dover Publications, 1956), chap. 4.
49. See Fr. Spiegel, *Eranische Altertumskunde* (1871), vol. 2, pp. 149 ff.
50. Leisegang, "The Mystery of the Serpent," p. 112.
51. *Malleus maleficarum* (Strassburg, 1487).
52. C. G. Jung, "Concerning the Self," trans. Hildegard Nagel, in *Spring 1951*: 1 ff. (A very similar translation by R. F. C. Hull is found in CW 9, ii, §§ 44–46.)
53. See Jung-Kerényi, *Essays on a Science of Mythology*, Bollingen Series 22 (Princeton: Princeton University Press, 1949), parts 3 and 4.
54. See in this connection ibid., pp. 158–60.
55. Toni Wolff, "A Few Thoughts on the Process of Individuation in Women," in *Spring 1941*: 90 ff.
56. *Essays on a Science of Mythology*, p. 172.
57. Von Salis, *Antike und Renaissance*, plate 56b, opposite p. 177.
58. *The Golden Ass*, trans. Robert Graves (Farrar, Straus & Giroux, 1951), chap. 19, pp. 284–85.
59. Ibid., chap. 18, p. 280.
60. C. G. Jung, CW 12, § 26.
61. Compare with C. G. Jung, CW 9, ii, §§ 347–421.

Publisher's Note

Gladys Phelan's translation from Linda Fierz-David's German manuscript was completed almost two and a half decades ago. Spring Publications gratefully acknowledges the help of Nor Hall, who worked with Miss Phelan's translation to bring a more contemporary phrasing to the language of the text. Spring Publications takes responsibility for this final copyedited version.

Gladys Phelan translated all the poetry. Spring Publications changed all C. G. Jung references to accord with standard form for the *Collected Works* (volume and paragraph numbers).

For Related Reading

DIONYSUS: MYTH AND CULT
Walter F. Otto

Possibly *the* classic work on the God, this book examines Dionysiac worship in the maenad cults, the mask, tragedy and theatre, in silence, pandaemonium and somber madness, through the vine and juices of vegetative nature, and in relation with woman, especially Ariadne. A full, authoritative phenomenology of Dionysus by a scholar whose understanding carries the reader into participation. Plates, notes, index. (xxi, 243 pp.)

FACING THE GODS
James Hillman, ed.

Among nine chapters showing how major figures of the Greek mythological imagination still work in the modern psyche are "Ariadne, Mistress of the Labyrinth" (Chris Downing) and "Dionysos in Jung's Writings" (James Hillman). Downing follows a serpentine way to connect myth and autobiography; Hillman shows how Jung conflated Wotan and Dionysos and connects the God's dismemberment with psyche's multiplicity. Notes, references, index. (172 pp.)

GODDESSES OF SUN AND MOON
Karl Kerényi

Restoring passionate feminine consciousness to its rightful place both in politics and in the economy of the psyche, these four papers explore the mythemes of Circe, Aphrodite, Niobe and Medea. Kerényi meditates on the puzzle of Medea, "the anti-Ariadne," who commits the dark and horrifying deeds of fratricide and infanticide while belonging to the Sun's family. (84 pp.)

THE DREAM OF POLIPHILO
Linda Fierz-David

This beautiful book (with 34 illustrations) is back in print after some thirty years. Fierz-David interprets the *Hypnerotomachia,* published in Venice during the Renaissance. The narrative recounts the dream of Poliphilo ("Lover of Polia") who is led by his beloved through a series of fantastic adventures in a legendary landscape. Polia, who speaks for the sensate spirit of the Renaissance, frees Poliphilo from his introverted obsession with alchemy and the medieval restrictions of courtly love. Led back into classical culture, he awakens transformed by the love of his guide, reconnected again to ancient humanism, its psychological depths and erotic wisdom. Foreword by C. G. Jung. (iii, 245 pp.)